PRAISE FOR *THE PLANT-BASED COOKBOOK*

"A plant-based diet not only helps with weight control, lowering cholesterol, and overall disease prevention; evidence shows that it also has the power to slow the progression of a surprising range of conditions, including multiple sclerosis. Take it from Ashley Madden, who faced her MS diagnosis head-on by learning about the power of nutrition for health. Ashley's cookbook will equip you with everything you need to know about stocking your pantry with plant-based ingredients, tips and tricks to save you time, and a wonderful selection of recipes that will have you questioning why you didn't try a plant-based diet sooner!"

—Neal Barnard, MD, FACC, Physicians Committee for Responsible Medicine

"Filled to the brim with timely and thoughtful information procured from Ashley's firsthand experience using food as medicine as a person living with multiple sclerosis. Ashley offers up an elegant and accessible celebration of whole foods making healthier foods taste amazing. *The Plant-Based Cookbook* gently invites its readers to see whole foods in a new way. This book will become a staple in kitchens for years to come, showcasing healthy recipes that don't compromise on taste!"

—Michael Greger, M.D. FACLM, founder of NutritionFacts.org and author of *How Not to Die*

"Ashley is a plant-based visionary! The ultimate guru when it comes to creating the healthiest, most vibrant, and flavorful meals! You'll want to make every recipe!"

—Chloe Coscarelli, vegan chef and author of *Chloe Flavor*

"With *The Plant-Based Cookbook*, Ashley Madden demonstrates how food lovers can have it all—optimize their health and enjoy delicious, nutritious cuisine. This informative and beautiful book will give you the confidence you need to make healthful meals. Ashley offers up a tasty variety of family-friendly, traditional, and unique recipes that anyone who loves to eat will appreciate."

—Julieanna Hever, Plant-Based Dietitian™, author of *The Healthspan Solution* and *Plant-Based Nutrition (Idiots Guide)*

"This cookbook is a delight! But it's not just a cookbook. Ashley Madden is absolutely inspirational in showing how plant-based cooking can not only produce sumptuous and delicious meals, but act, as it has for her, as a recipe for robust good health, even for those with serious chronic illness."

—Professor George Jelinek, MD MBBS, Dip DHM FACEM, author of *Overcoming Multiple Sclerosis*

"*The Plant-Based Cookbook* is bursting with brilliant dinner ideas, colorful salads, wholesome breakfast alternatives, and guilt-free sweets! Ashley has a talent for expanding the reader's view of food, no matter their personal journey. Because of Ashley, I cook oil-free and gluten-free with confidence, something I never imagined being able to do. This book is full of gorgeous photos and inspiring recipes that anyone who likes good food will appreciate."

—Dustin Harder, chef, author, television host, and creator of *The Vegan Roadie*

"Gorgeous, delectable, and mouthwatering are just a few of the adjectives to aptly describe *The Plant-Based Cookbook* from Ashley Madden. I found myself turning the pages and saying 'Ohhh, I want that!' more times than I can count. Her easy-to-follow recipes combined with healing plant-based ingredients offer an approachable and nourishing feast for the senses. This book is going to inspire the curious foodie to explore the myriad benefits of a plant-based lifestyle and also offer newfound culinary inspiration to seasoned cooks with its vibrant recipes and health-supporting information."

—Jason Wrobel, celebrity vegan chef, cooking channel TV host, and co-founder of Wellevatr

The
PLANT-BASED
COOKBOOK

Vegan, Gluten-Free, Oil-Free Recipes for Lifelong Health

ASHLEY MADDEN

B.Sc.(Pharm), ACPR, C.H.N.

Skyhorse Publishing

Copyright © 2021 by Ashley Madden
Photography © 2021 by Ashley Madden

All rights reserved. No part of this book may be reproduced in any manner without the express written consent of the publisher, except in the case of brief excerpts in critical reviews or articles. All inquiries should be addressed to Skyhorse Publishing, 307 West 36th Street, 11th Floor, New York, NY 10018.

Skyhorse Publishing books may be purchased in bulk at special discounts for sales promotion, corporate gifts, fund-raising, or educational purposes. Special editions can also be created to specifications. For details, contact the Special Sales Department, Skyhorse Publishing, 307 West 36th Street, 11th Floor, New York, NY 10018 or info@skyhorsepublishing.com.

Skyhorse® and Skyhorse Publishing® are registered trademarks of Skyhorse Publishing, Inc.®, a Delaware corporation.

Visit our website at www.skyhorsepublishing.com.

10 9 8 7 6 5 4 3

Library of Congress Cataloging-in-Publication Data is available on file.

Cover design by Daniel Brount
Cover photo by Ashley Madden

Print ISBN: 978-1-5107-5761-5
Ebook ISBN: 978-1-5107-5762-2

Printed in China

Dedicated to Bernard.
For believing in my dreams and chasing them with me. For your endless support
and for eating everything I've ever cooked. (Except for that curry in 2011.)
I love you.

CONTENTS

Introduction   ix

My Story: From Prescriptions to Plants   xiii

Part I: A New Food Philosophy   1

The Essentials: Kitchen Tools & the Plant-Based Pantry   11

Cooking & Preparation Methods   24

Tips, Tricks & Shortcuts   29

Part II: Recipes   32

Breakfast Bowls, Blends & Brunch   34

The Breakfast Bakery   58

Soups & Stews   79

Sensational Salads   104

Dips & Spreads   129

Plantiful Plates & Bowls   147

Sweets & Treats   211

Menus for Any Occasion   245

Inspiration, Education & Resources   247

Acknowledgments   251

Conversion Charts   253

Index   254

INTRODUCTION

With great challenge comes great change. I don't know where I read that, but it's proven to be true over and over again my own life. And these challenges, no matter how unwelcome or painful, can help you shift and reshape your life for the better. If you let them. If you *embrace* rather than resist.

In the middle of my own quarter-life calamity (ahem, personal shit storm), I realized I was going through major life-altering change and transformation. Like so many people, maybe you included, I had to get sick in order to appreciate health. I remember sitting in a bare hospital room, a heartbreaking diagnosis still echoing in my ears, and questioning for the first time what a healthy lifestyle really looked like.

From that moment onward, my personal and professional life would change forever. And over the next decade a new food philosophy and approach to health would emerge. One shaped by my career as a pharmacist, my education in holistic nutrition, my training as a chef, my love (capital L) of food, and, last but certainly not least, my diagnosis of multiple sclerosis at the age of twenty-three.

If I were to neatly summarize what I've learned over the last fifteen years, it would be that the old health adages were telling us everything we need to know: food is medicine, we are what we eat, an ounce of prevention is worth a pound of cure. Not overly exciting, not earth-shattering news. But that's the problem, it's almost unbelievable. It's a message that's simple and straightforward yet often dressed up as complicated and convoluted.

"Eat food. Not too much. Mostly plants." As Michael Pollan, author of *In Defense of Food*, so eloquently said. You can capture this idea a handful of different ways: shop the perimeter, an apple a day, and my personal favorite, eat the rainbow! These trending hashtags point to the common denominator in any healthy diet: eat more whole, plant-based foods and fewer processed ones. Does that stir something within you? Does it ring true for you as it does for me?

If you've purchased this book or you're flipping through the pages, chances are you're interested in making some changes, improving your diet, preparing more meatless meals, or even just learning more about whole foods.

Listen to your intuition. Consider that what you eat is one of the most important decisions you make throughout your life, every day, multiple times a day. And you get to decide again, and again. Food is profoundly important.

Unfortunately, there's not one perfect diet for everyone, and dietary needs shift throughout life and under different circumstances. But I wholeheartedly believe that most of us can benefit from moving toward a diet focused on vegetables, fruits, whole grains, and legumes—even if it's just a tiny step in that direction. No matter what your diet looks like right now, know that making the choice to eat more whole foods will change your life. Period.

Whether you consider yourself an omnivore or vegan, Michelin star chef or an amateur home cook, I hope this cookbook and my story help you move forward in your health and culinary journey to a place where food inspires joy, healing, and creativity.

Throughout these pages you'll find a collection of my favorite plant-based, whole-food recipes, as well as nutritional and culinary tips. My goal is to motivate you to see your plate and bowl in a new and optimistic way. It's how we eat in our house, and it's a lifestyle that has helped me heal in ways that extend far beyond my physical health.

I'm not a doctor nor an expert in your dietary needs. But through my work as a clinical pharmacist, holistic nutritionist, and cooking instructor, I've seen, up close and personal, how this way of eating can revolutionize lives.

I should add this: You don't need to be knowledgeable in health and wellness or a trained chef to make nourishing, satisfying meals. You don't need to sprout buckwheat or juice wheatgrass to create a health supportive kitchen (wonderful things, but not required!). You can live a full life and still get a wholesome meal on the table at the end of the day without relying on packaged foods or loads of foreign ingredients.

When I was diagnosed with MS, I didn't know how to cook rice or even bake a potato (seriously). My preferred method of cooking involved the microwave. I never, ever, imagined that one day I would write a cookbook about how the gripping fear of chronic disease can lead to an empowering lifestyle and whole-foods diet.

At my core I believe a plant-based kitchen is one that supports wellness in all areas of your life. It's a space for connection, enjoyment, and exploration.

It's messy and busy and definitely, positively, not perfect. It might force you to slow down and get your hands dirty, and that's a good thing.

Without realizing it, I returned to wellness in my kitchen. In fact, I discovered wellness in my kitchen.

And so can you.

I'm grateful for and humbled by the opportunities I've been given and by the challenges that lead to great change—and to this book you're holding.

This is my plant-based kitchen. Welcome ❤

MY STORY
FROM PRESCRIPTIONS
TO PLANTS

Clarification: I'm not suggesting anyone stop taking prescription medications! I am however pressing rewind because I couldn't write this cookbook without sharing how I got here—from pharmacist to plant-based chef.

It's 2008 and I'm twenty-three. I've just graduated from pharmacy school. I'm stressed out and high-strung but consider myself healthy (at least healthy-ish). Chronic back pain leads to an MRI, and in my follow-up appointment (on Valentine's Day, to be exact) I'm told I have multiple sclerosis (MS).

Time stood still.

For what it's worth, the back pain was unrelated to my diagnosis. If you're unfamiliar with MS, it's an incurable neurological autoimmune disease where the immune system attacks and destroys nerve fibers in your brain, causing symptoms or loss of function throughout the body. The body parts or systems affected depend on what areas of the brain and spinal cord are involved. Prognosis is generally impossible to predict. Instead, you're left with a lot of what-ifs and hypothetical situations. In other words, fear.

Faced with the possibility of disability, an unknown future, and contemplating for the first time my own mortality, I began to question everything. *Everything*! My life, career, relationships, you name it. The existential questions came fast and furious—who am I, what's life about, what do I want? The aftermath of the diagnosis ushered in a quarter-life catastrophe.

Having an aunt who died with MS coupled with my superficial understanding of the disease made acceptance painful and emotional. Shortly after I was diagnosed, my sister was too. It was no longer just about me, it was us. Looking back, I see that I had to cycle through the stages of grief before I was ready to face reality.

Gradually, I started to think about what I could do to change the trajectory of my health. I didn't want to just inject myself with drugs and hope for the best. So, as a true student of academia, I devoted myself to research. While I worked as a pharmacist in the day, I was like a secret agent at night reading everything I could about MS. Which quickly expanded to reading about more common modern-day chronic diseases like cancer, cardiovascular disease, and diabetes. I was highlighting and taking notes. I had an investigative fever. I wasn't just a practitioner anymore; I was a patient.

Even as a practicing pharmacist, I was surprised to learn about the rise of chronic disease, sickness, and morbidity that was plaguing the developed world. Didn't we have this under control with drugs and modern medicine? Where were the experimental drugs and quick fixes?

As I read everything with new eyes, I recognized that the connection between diet and disease and longevity was ubiquitous. Small pockets of forward-thinking healthcare professionals were revisiting the foundation of basic health and disease prevention and trying to get their message heard. It became clear that diet and health were tightly woven together. The lines between food and disease prevention blurred.

Could it be that simple and complex? Was food *that* important?

I need to point out here that I believe, without question, that medicine is necessary. I support and rely on doctors, pharmacists, prescriptions, and evidence-based research. And yes, modern medicine ensures we live longer . . . but a lot of us are also living sicker. In 2020 the U.S. Centers for Disease Control and Prevention (CDC) stated that "6 in 10 Americans live with at least one chronic disease." Poor diet and unhealthy lifestyles are listed as the main contributors to this staggering statistic.

Accumulating scientific research, anecdotal evidence, and simple common sense have identified the problems with our current, Westernized diet—mainly that processed foods, refined sugars, inflammatory fats, and excessive intake of animal products have replaced nutrient-rich, whole foods. Somewhere along the way we traded wholesome for convenience and confused authentic with artificial. Frozen low-calorie dinners and powdered breakfast shakes were proof that I had fallen victim to this broken, modern-day food machine.

Once I absorbed and digested (pun fully intended) all of this information, I made a decision to take responsibility for my health. I adopted a whole-food, plant-based, crap-free diet. As I redefined my personal life, I felt a similar distancing from my pharmacy profession. Like a reflex, change in one prompted change in the other. Food became my obsession. What started as an effort to prevent progression of my MS became a fascination with how the food we eat can prevent some of the deadliest diseases plaguing the developed world.

I began studying holistic nutrition and devoured the stack of books that showed up at my door. I studied micronutrients in detail, learned about the fallout of poor digestion, and considered the healing power of plants. I started to see the most common health problems through a new lens.

Ultimately, I traded prescriptions for plants in my personal and professional life. Having almost a decade's worth of experience as a health professional, I was fully aware of the shortcomings of Western medicine but could also interpret my holistic health lessons with a grain of salt. I had perspective and understood how the two were more complementary than in opposition to each other.

As I learned more about the connection between food and health, I was drawn to the kitchen. I committed myself to including more fruits and vegetables in my diet. It started with adding a handful of spinach to a smoothie. Then making burgers out of beans and sauces out of pureed vegetables. I was shocked at how delicious whole foods could be. Soon after, I found myself in midtown Manhattan on my first day of culinary school at the Natural Gourmet Institute—New York's leading health culinary institute at that time.

Culinary school was where I put the pieces together. I learned how to properly handle produce, how to simmer, sauté, and broil. I learned how to make traditional sauces, galettes, and infused oils. It was wonderful . . . but I couldn't help but put my spin on recipes. I'd ask our instructors if we could bake instead of fry our quinoa croquettes and sub water for oil in our pistachio pesto. I easily saw the ways in which we could make meals healthier by replacing ingredients or altering cooking methods. This might have been culinary blasphemy, but I had a different approach to food. Once and for all, I was certain that food could taste amazing and still be exceptionally health supportive.

I couldn't accept anything less.

While living in New York, I was also lucky enough to intern for the fabulous and ever-inspiring Chloe Coscarelli, famed vegan chef and multiple cookbook author. I learned more about vegan recipe testing, being an entrepreneur, and pursuing your passion!

After culinary school I was bursting with inspiration and wanted to share all the information I had gathered. I started my website RiseShineCook.ca as a place to share my recipes and healthy cooking techniques. And in the years that followed I would do everything from plant-based cooking classes, one-on-one consulting, pop-up bake sales, corporate talks, and writing for health magazines and wellness websites. Documenting my recipes meant learning about photography, and now I'm also a freelance food photographer.

During that time, my husband and I moved around the world from Canada to the Netherlands and Taiwan, and we've traveled many places in between. What's clear in every place I've lived is that people everywhere and of all walks of life are waking up to the sobering state of our nutritional well-being. People like you are educating themselves and opting for healthier cookbooks and holistic approaches to health care.

I know that I'm meant to help others on their journey to health in the kitchen. It's my purpose and my passion. I practice what I preach and am determined to show you how easy and incredibly life-changing a whole-food, plant-based diet can be.

PART I
A NEW FOOD PHILOSOPHY

This book isn't about convincing you to give up meat or persuading you to throw out all the oils in your cupboard (although there are a few you should 100 percent throw out). Rather, it's about exploring your options to choose these ways of eating because of how they make you feel, how it can benefit your health (and the planet), and still satisfy your taste buds.

All of the recipes in this book are vegan, plant-based, and gluten-free, with no added oils and a focus on anti-inflammatory and whole-food ingredients. I believe the more we're all educated on the healing power of foods and their ability to prevent common health problems, the more we will choose these very foods as part of our daily dietary habits.

When I originally set out to change my own diet, I found many "healthy" recipes that compromised here or there, like a healthy stir-fry made with just a glug of vegetable oil or a vegan cupcake stuffed with processed margarine. These good-intentioned recipes motivated me to

> **Nutritional Nugget**
> Inflammation is a necessary process required for healing and repair throughout the body. However, when inflammation becomes chronic, it can cause problems, contributing to serious health issues like heart disease, arthritis, and cancer. There are two key features of an anti-inflammatory diet.
>
> - *Consuming anti-inflammatory foods*: These are foods containing antioxidants and other compounds that fight or mitigate inflammation in our bodies. This includes most whole, plant-based foods. Berries, flax seeds, and dark leafy greens are especially anti-inflammatory.
> - *Avoiding inflammation-causing foods*: To establish an overall anti-inflammatory diet it's also important to avoid foods that cause inflammation. These include refined carbohydrates and sugars, animal products, soda, and deep-fried or highly processed foods.

bring vegetarian and vegan cooking one step further.

I began creating the recipes I was looking for.

With determination and a lot (*a lot*) of experimentation (and a husband willing to eat just about anything), I found ways to skip processed oils in everyday cooking. I replaced refined flours in gluten-free baked goods, and made milks, cheeses, and ice creams without using any dairy. This was during a time when vegan and gluten-free eating was considered very fringe and "hippie."

Instead of searching for new ingredients, I just reinvented how we used familiar ones; all without relying on seemingly "healthy" plant-based commercial ingredients like soy-based cheeses, uber-refined sugars, or vegan butters.

These are the recipes you'll find in this book—one-pot meals, casseroles, cozy soups, and decadent desserts for special occasions. Plant-based does not have to be synonymous with boring, bland, or high maintenance. Health-supportive eating can be elegant, effortless, and enjoyable. I promise.

Naturally, when I decided to change my diet and lifestyle, I feared I'd have to give up meals I loved, and that food would no longer be a source of joy, fun, or comfort. (Reminder—I *love* food.) If you have similar hesitations, let me tell you that the opposite happened! I enjoy my food now more than ever. You might be thinking that I've obviously forgotten how bacon tastes. (I haven't.) Eating whole foods has upgraded my culinary experience a million-fold. I eat often and until I'm full and I never ever feel deprived. I've come to learn that this is a common discovery among most people who opt for a plant-based lifestyle.

I tell you this before I get into some food principles I follow because I want to be clear that a whole-food, plant-based diet is not one of deprivation, scarcity, or bland and boring food. Au contraire, health foodie friend, the plant-based kitchen you're about to enter is abundant, flavorful, and exciting.

The following food philosophy, a collection of guidelines if you will, is one developed from my health education and own personal experiences. I encourage you to keep an open mind, try new things, and to explore what resonates with you. Remember, we're all different. Some of you might feel better avoiding nightshade vegetables, soy, or cashews. Some people can't tolerate sugar, even natural forms or small amounts, and others have difficulty digesting raw vegetables. It's up to you to learn what works and makes you feel good—maybe leading to your own food philosophy! Once you figure it out, it might change again. This is the journey of living in a human body—we're all unique and we change and grow (if we're lucky!) and so do our needs.

Your food journey is unique to you. Honor it. Having a health-supportive kitchen means recognizing that the food you buy, prepare, and eat is directly related to your energy, longevity, and quality of life. Start where you are and know that it's never too late to make health-inspired changes. Health is available to all of us. It starts in the kitchen and tastes all kinds of delicious.

With that said, let's get down to it.

Whole Foods, Plant Based

A whole-food, plant-based diet has at its foundation unrefined, unprocessed plants. These plants are generally divided into the following food groups: vegetables, fruits, whole grains, legumes (beans and peas), nuts, and seeds. These foods are versatile and provide endless options for meal planning and recipe creation.

When it comes to whole foods, nutrient density is an important concept to understand.

> **Nutrient density** refers to the ratio of nutrients per calorie of food. The more nutrients per calorie the more nutrient dense a food is considered.

Alternatively, the terms "empty calories" or "calorie density" refer to foods that provide a lot of calories and fewer nutrients.

A mind-blowing realization for me was that calories without nutrients can lead to cravings and overeating. Of course! Even if our bodies receive enough energy in the form of calories, they still want and need nutrients—fiber, minerals, vitamins—and so we feel the need to keep eating. Plant-based foods are nutrient dense and filling—win-win. Whole foods provide us with macronutrients (carbs, fat, protein) and micronutrients (vitamins, minerals, and incredible phytonutrients!).

Fiber is another plant-based asset. Fiber, which cannot be broken down by the human digestive system, helps with digestion, keeps us full longer, can stabilize blood sugar, and lower cholesterol. Health Canada suggests that women get 25 grams of fiber daily and men 38 grams. But most people don't even get half that!

> **Phytonutrients** are nutrients produced by and found in plants. There are thousands of phytonutrients, most of which have not been studied, and some that may still be unidentified. Frequently discussed phytonutrients include beta-carotene, lycopene, anthocyanin, and resveratrol. Different phytonutrients are represented by different colors meaning the new age "eat the rainbow" adage is derived from the wisdom that a variety of colorful foods will provide a wide range of plant nutrients whose benefits go beyond our knowledge. Phytonutrients make foods nutritious!

And guess what? Fiber only comes from plants. You won't get any fiber from animal products. And most processed foods have the fiber removed.

> ### More Fiber, Less Cholesterol
> Take a moment to think about this. Plants provide fiber and have zero cholesterol whereas animal products introduce cholesterol into our diets and provide zero fiber.

Plant-Based Food Groups
Vegetables & Fruit
There is no overestimating how important fruits and veggies are to our health. The World Health Organization has stated that inadequate intake of fruits and vegetables contributed to almost 4 million deaths worldwide in 2017.

Fruits and vegetables are absolutely essential to overall health and I suggest trying to include them in every single meal (especially leafy greens). As a rule, I aim for 1 to 2 cups of raw or cooked vegetables with lunch and dinner either as a side salad or steamed (or as part of a recipe).

Whole Grains
Whole grains, like brown rice, and pseudo grains, like quinoa and buckwheat, are a major component of a whole-foods diet. These provide B vitamins, vitamin E, iron, magnesium, and fiber. They're extremely satisfying and satiating. And because they're so important, it's essential to understand the difference between a whole grain and refined grain.

Legumes

Legumes, also known as pulses, are the edible mature seeds of plants. They include beans, peas, lentils, soybeans, and peanuts. Beans have been labeled one of the most important predictors of survival around the globe, so I say eat beans to live longer! Legumes are supremely nutritious, offering protein, complex carbohydrates, fiber, phytonutrients, vitamins, and minerals in addition to being low in fat and free from cholesterol (like every plant, by the way!). They also help regulate digestion and increase satiation. Legumes are a dietary staple in cultures all around the world and I think one of the most underutilized food groups. See page 27 for instructions on how to cook beans.

Nuts & Seeds

Nuts and seeds are tremendously beneficial for our health! They're nutrient and calorie dense and are the largest source of fat in a plant-based diet. Because of this, they represent a smaller portion of a plant-based diet, but a little goes a long way. I like to keep an assortment of raw nuts and seeds on hand at all times and use them to make creamy sauces, piecrusts, and pantry seasonings. For special occasions, a nut-based cheese ball or cheesecake can impress the pants off any plant-based naysayers.

I recommend only buying unroasted, unsalted nuts. The healthy fats in nuts can oxidize and lose much of their benefit over time when exposed to heat, light, and oxygen. For this reason, it's important to store fresh nuts in sealed containers in the fridge or freezer.

Processed Foods versus Whole Foods

Inherent to the notion of a whole-foods, plant-based diet is the omission or minimal use of processed foods. Processed foods are foods that have been manipulated or altered from their original form in some way or another. Not all processed foods are unhealthy, and it's important to understand that processed foods exist on a continuum ranging from minimally processed to extremely processed.

In my kitchen, I try to use minimally processed foods as much as is possible and practical (and what's practical will change depending on your lifestyle and priorities). The problem lies in the fact that we have gradually broadened our acceptance of what qualifies as actual food. We've accepted food wannabes into our diet and we've even allowed them to replace the real, authentic foods that we need.

The abundance of food products that now populate our supermarkets is remarkable. Some items like dried grains and legumes, bottled spices, and frozen fruits have made healthy eating more accessible but others (read: most) are nothing but a whisper of the original food or recipe from which they were inspired.

Cake mixes, frozen family dinners, crackers, cookies, and sauces—these highly processed foods have introduced us to lists of artificial ingredients and have taken up serious real estate in our diets. This is a major, five-alarm-fire health problem.

Processed foods are cheap to make and allow for an extended shelf life, which is great for food manufacturers but not so much for us. They expose us to refined carbohydrates and sugar, excess amounts of sodium, inflammatory oils, trans fats, and foreign chemicals.

Processed foods are jeopardizing our health in ways we don't fully understand. No matter what it says on the box, no matter the promise made by a particular product, if it has a long ingredient list that looks more like a science project than a recipe, or if it has sugar or oil in any form as the first three ingredients, you're better off leaving it out of your cart.

No/Low-Oil Cooking

All of my home cooking is done without any added oils. For me this was an easy decision, and although it's a personal preference, I want to share my reasons. First, bottled vegetable oils are responsible for much of the dietary inflammation in our modern-day diets. These oils are high in omega-6 inflammatory fats, are uber refined, and expose us to fat-soluble, industrial toxins. Most oils stocking grocery store shelves have already gone rancid.

Second, oils aren't whole foods. They provide predominantly one nutrient—fat. Any health benefits available from these oils are also available from the whole food along with fiber, complementary nutrients, and active enzymes. The whole food provides the whole package and allows for optimal nutrition. This argument can also be applied to maple syrup for example (which I use) but whereas maple syrup is used rather infrequently or in small amounts, oils tend to be used daily and in excess. I also recognize that oil-free is more accurately described as no added oils, because whole foods naturally contain oil.

Third, I don't feel as though cooking with oils is necessary! Sautéing vegetables in water and using whole foods to make salad dressings has served me well. Last, and this is a very personal reason, research has shown that a diet low in saturated fat has the potential to slow (or even prevent) progression of MS and decrease risk factors for many common chronic illnesses. Oils are high in fat and many high in saturated fat

(especially coconut oil and coconut products).

For me, eliminating oils when cooking was easier than even using them sparingly and fit nicely with my other conclusions about oil. I understand that there are different approaches to this topic, and I know that oils are considered essential in some cuisines, but I invite you to try replacing oils as I do in my recipes even if just for fun or out of curiosity.

Please note that by oil-free, I don't mean fat-free! I like to include whole-food sources of fat like nuts, seeds, and avocados regularly in my recipes. And here I'm also referring to oils used when cooking and not for medical treatment or therapeutic purposes. I know that for many inflammatory conditions, essential fatty acid oils and supplements are used as part of treatment plans.

You'll discover that oil-free cooking is low maintenance, easy, and cheap! There are no complex methods that you'll have to master, but I'll review how I replace oils on page 25. With the guiding principles of eating whole foods, decreasing inflammatory omega-6 exposure, reducing dietary free radicals, and keeping fat and calorie intake in check, I choose to reduce oils in most of my food preparation.

Vegan

As I learned more about the importance of whole foods, digestion, and calorie density, I naturally moved away from animal products. When I became more educated in nutritional science and the association between animal products and cancer, cardiovascular disease, and chronic inflammation, I knew that animal products would no longer be a part of my diet.

A vegan diet free from animal products appealed to me initially for health reasons but then extended to compassion for animals and a desire to heal our planet and combat climate change. Eating a vegan diet has been a freeing and rewarding lifestyle choice. Really. It feels so good.

Ultimately, labels don't matter, and the diet that works best for you does not need to fit in a predefined box, but for transparency and to help you navigate the grocery aisles, I would like to take a moment to clarify that vegan and plant-based diets aren't the same thing. A vegan diet can certainly be one that is based on whole, minimally processed foods but isn't by definition. Potato chips and soda are technically vegan and there is no shortage of vegan junk food available. I avidly and passionately support the vegan movement in its entirety, and I think that any step away from animal products is in the right direction, but choosing foods solely based on a vegan label doesn't always guarantee a healthy option.

Gluten-Free

With the rise of non-celiac gluten sensitivity and awareness of gluten intolerance, many people are seeking gluten- and wheat-free recipes. There's also evidence that some types of autoimmune diseases respond well to a gluten-free diet. For these reasons and to accommodate anyone eliminating gluten or with celiac disease (who must give up gluten!), my recipes are completely gluten-free.

Having said that, I don't believe everyone needs to avoid gluten. It's become a popular trend and can do more harm than good if not done correctly. Gluten-free packaged foods line grocery shelves everywhere and many of these products replace gluten with processed sugars, fats, and artificial ingredients. Most commercial gluten-free foods are very (read: dangerously) unhealthy.

If you're following a gluten-free diet, be extra cautious of gluten-free packaged and premade foods and if you're not gluten-free, none of these recipes will require any extra special gluten-free products. Gluten will be replaced in my recipes with fiber-rich grains and other whole foods providing healthier gluten-free options.

> **If you're not gluten-free, you can still easily make all these recipes.** Simply use regular oats instead of gluten-free, regular soy sauce or shoyu instead of tamari, and whole wheat pasta, as opposed to brown rice or quinoa.

Imperfection

A guiding principle I teach with respect to a plant-based diet is the importance of an open-minded, compassionate, and curious approach to making changes and trying new recipes. Striving for a perfect diet or acting from a place of restriction and fear, as opposed to acceptance and optimism, can be stressful and discouraging. I know because I've been there! Changing your diet and how you see your plate is a process and there are always new things to learn.

I'm learning new stuff all the time! As I age and as my needs shift, the way I do things, the foods I want to eat, and the recipes I love change too. Give yourself this freedom as well and please approach mealtime with an easygoing attitude. "Perfect" is an illusion in every area of life and, if I'm being honest, it's boring. Show up in your kitchen as you are with all your quirks, and you'll make these recipes your own and they'll be better off for it, and so will you! Start where you are, and you'll get where you're going.

THE ESSENTIALS
KITCHEN TOOLS & THE PLANT-BASED PANTRY

Tools

In my experience the difference between someone who cooks and someone who doesn't is equipment and supplies. How can you take on any task if you don't have the tools you need? This is not a totally inclusive list, but these are my most used and needed kitchen gear outside of pots, pans, cutting boards, measuring cups and spoons, and knives.

Blender: The most-used small appliance in my kitchen is my blender. I use a Vitamix because it's a powerful, game-changing machine capable of pureeing whole foods into sauces and dips and whipping up creamy smoothies. It's the Beyoncé of blenders! It's certainly an investment but one you won't regret. I also like to use a smaller blender for small-batch sauces. Newer blenders at cheaper price points are hitting the market all the time. Browse around and see what's available.

Food processor: A food processor is equally important in creating delicious plant-based meals like burgers, bliss balls, and bean dips. You can find a great food processor for an affordable price. I suggest getting a 12-cup container and skipping the fancy accessories.

Dishers and spring-release scoops: Use these for easy measuring and

> ### Tip: Dishers
> How to get that perfectly shaped muffin, cookie, or bean ball? Scoops! Inexpensive stainless-steel scoops with a spring release, also known as dishers, are useful tools to have in the kitchen. They can be found online or at restaurant supply stores. I use a ¾-fluid-ounce scoop (#40 disher) for cookies, bliss balls, and bean balls and a 3¼-ounce scoop (#10 disher) for muffins and bean burgers throughout the book.

shaping of cookies, bean burgers, muffins, and bliss balls!

Steaming basket: I have steamed vegetables almost every evening. A steamer basket is cheap and easy to use. I bought mine for less than five bucks.

Microplane: This is a fine grater that can zest lemons but is also great for finely grating fresh ginger.

Box grater: I use this to grate any vegetable by hand. Inexpensive and useful.

Nut-milk bag: This is a mesh bag that is used to strain nut and seed milks. They're inexpensive and last a long time.

Fine-mesh strainer: These are inexpensive and ideal for rinsing grains and straining broths or soups.

Large nonstick sauté pan: This makes sautéing without oil and cooking pancakes much easier. There are many brands and types and lots of reviews to peruse on the Internet.

Silicone baking pans: I use silicone donut, muffin, and bread pans interchangeably with traditional baking pans. They're easy to clean and make oil-free baking even easier.

Spiralizer or julienne peeler: Being able to turn whole foods into noodles still fascinates me. I like to spiralize zucchini for a fresh and crisp side dish or in place of pasta. A good julienne peeler can also create the same effect.

Plant-Based Pantry

Having a well-stocked and organized pantry will make healthy cooking a breeze! Here I want to highlight new or unique ingredients and some things you might not have used up until now. I'll explain what they are, where to find them, and what you'll use them for.

Whole Grains

Considering whole grains are the foundation of many of my recipes, I want to make sure we're all on the same page. Here are the ones I use most often.

Brown rice: Brown rice is my go-to grain. It doesn't need much explanation other than I use two varieties—short-grain brown rice and long-grain brown rice. Short-grain brown rice is a little stickier and chewier, and long-grain brown rice is fluffier and the grains stay separated. Brown rice, depending on the variety, takes between 35 and 45 minutes to cook. I don't use minute rice or fast cooking rice brands in my recipes.

Quinoa: Quinoa has reached superfood status and for good reason. It's a great source of fiber, vitamins, minerals, and, most notably, protein. Quinoa, which is actually a seed, provides complete protein, meaning it contains all nine essential amino acids. Quinoa takes less than 15 minutes to prepare and needs to be rinsed in water before cooking to remove a natural substance called saponin, which has a bitter, unpalatable flavor. I prefer white quinoa for its fluffy texture and flavor, but red and black quinoa are also available.

Buckwheat: Buckwheat is actually a pseudo-grain related to the rhubarb plant. Raw buckwheat groats have had their outer husks removed to reveal a light-colored, pyramid-shaped "grain." Buckwheat is available raw or toasted, known as kasha. I generally opt for raw buckwheat and have come to love its earthy flavor, which lends itself perfectly to baked goods and raw porridges. You can find buckwheat groats in most health food stores or online. Despite having "wheat" in its name, buckwheat is wheat- and gluten-free.

Rolled oats: Rolled oats are technically processed but minimally—the oat groats are dehulled, steamed, and rolled. They show up a lot in my baked goods, breakfast recipes, and bean burgers. Most oats are not gluten-free, because they're processed in the same factories as wheat but there are certain manufacturers that produce specifically gluten-free brands (see page 249 for resources). If avoiding gluten is essential for you, ensure you have certified gluten-free oats. I use old-fashioned, gluten-free rolled oats in all my recipes (not quick-cooking oats).

Legumes

Beans, peas, and lentils come in dried and canned forms. Your local bulk store will have a nice selection. If you're used to buying canned beans, I strongly suggest you try cooking them at home—it's much cheaper and allows you to control the added salt. If you like to have a few cans on hand, as I do in the case of culinary emergencies, choose BPA-free brands.

Unless otherwise stated, most dried beans need to be soaked and then cooked. See page 27 for instructions on how to cook beans. Note that beans are often interchangeable in recipes, especially soups and stews.

Red lentils cook quickly and disintegrate to make thick soups and sauces. They're well known for their use in making Indian cuisine. Red lentils cannot be interchanged with brown and green lentils. Split peas don't hold their shape either. These are the legumes you'll find in this book:

- Adzuki beans
- Black beans
- Chickpeas
- Edamame
- Green peas
- Brown and green lentils
- Split red lentils
- Navy beans
- Cannellini beans
- Split yellow peas

Flours & Baking

My baking pantry is probably one of the most transformed areas of my kitchen. Where once stood all-purpose white flours is now whole grain, nutrient-dense flours—some of which I make myself!

Gluten-free baking is notoriously difficult, because without gluten it's hard to achieve the stretch and bounce of traditional breads or flakiness of piecrusts. I don't try to mimic any of these textures, and I don't get wrapped up in using commercial flour blends and refined starches (except arrowroot). Instead, I like to keep it really simple with the grain and nut flours listed. I also keep all my flours, especially the ones I grind myself, in the fridge to maintain freshness.

Oat flour: This is my preferred flour for muffins and breads. You can make this yourself by adding rolled oats to a blender or food processor and processing until a flour-like texture is achieved. Transfer the flour to a sealed container and keep it in the fridge.

Making Oat Flour

Generally, 1 cup of oats processed will provide ¾ cup oat flour. This also depends on how finely you blend the oats and the type of oats you use. I suggest always measuring the actual flour.

Buckwheat flour: I use 100 percent whole-grain buckwheat flour in my recipes. This flour is made with whole buckwheat groats and has visible black flecks of ground hull. This is a heavier, more flavorful, and nutritious flour. You can find buckwheat flour in health food stores, the organic aisles of most grocery stores,

and online. Similar to oat flour, you can also make your own buckwheat flour by processing buckwheat groats in a blender or food processor until a flour-like texture is achieved.

Brown rice flour: Brown rice flour is lighter in color and has a subtle flavor. It's a versatile flour that I also use as a thickener. Brown rice flour is best found in the organic or health section of most grocery stores.

Almond flour: Almond flour has a coarse texture and is made by grinding blanched almonds. I usually purchase mine from bulk food stores and keep it in the freezer. Note that it's best to remove it from the freezer an hour or so before using so the flour is less clumpy. Almond meal is also available, which is made from un-blanched almonds. While some recipes are best made with almond flour, almond meal can also be used in things like muffins, breads, or burgers without issue.

Psyllium husk: Psyllium husk is a magical baking ingredient. A soluble fiber derived from a plant, it has the ability to absorb water and create a mucilaginous texture which acts as a binder in baked goods. Like ground flax seeds, it can act as an egg replacer. Psyllium is available as whole psyllium husk or psyllium powder. Although they're not the same, they're interchangeable where 3 teaspoons of whole husk are equivalent to 2½ teaspoons of powder. You can find psyllium in most health food stores and online.

Arrowroot starch: Arrowroot starch, also known as arrowroot powder or flour, is a starch made from the arrowroot plant. It's a healthier (and my preferred) alternative to cornstarch. It's odorless, flavorless, and naturally gluten-free. Like cornstarch, it's used as a thickening agent but is much less processed and refined. I like to use arrowroot starch to thicken sauces but also in baked goods for texture and binding. Arrowroot starch mixed with cold liquid is known as a slurry. This slurry thickens when heated. Please note that if an arrowroot slurry is cooked at too high a temperature or for too long, it can "break" and lose its thickening properties. You can find arrowroot in the health food section or organic sections of most grocery stores.

Soy
Soy is definitely a loaded topic—one I'm not going to tackle it its entirety.

Whole books and associations are dedicated to soy and its impact on our health. From hormone imbalance to genetically modified organisms (GMO) to estrogen sensitive cancers, there's still disagreement. After working in cancer care as a pharmacist, after reading endless articles about soy and its impacts on health, after living and cooking in different countries and getting familiar with other culinary traditions, I choose to include minimally processed, organic soy products in my diet. If you also use soy products, I suggest always buying organic and non-GMO. I don't use processed soy foods or soy spinoffs like textured vegetable protein, soy cream cheese, soy bacon, sausages, or burgers. Here are the soy products in my kitchen.

Tempeh: Tempeh is made by fermenting soybeans and then packing them into rectangular cakes. Tempeh is rough and bumpy in texture with varying spots of discoloration. It's often fermented with whole grains like brown rice or millet. I love tempeh's earthy taste, hearty texture, and nutritional profile. It's a fantastic source of complete protein, fiber, probiotics (gut-healthy nutrients), and iron. Keep tempeh in your fridge (noting its expiration date) or freeze for up to three months. Tempeh is found in the refrigerated section in most health food sections of the grocery store.

Miso: Miso is a paste made from fermented soybeans. It's tangy and cheesy and gives food what is known as umami flavor—a fifth taste used to describe strong, savory foods like mushrooms or foods with glutamic acid. Miso is available in different varieties, but I predominantly use mellow or white miso (also known as shiro miso). Chickpea miso is now widely available and can be used instead of soybean miso if preferred.

Extra-firm and firm tofu: Tofu is made by blending soybeans with water, then adding a coagulant (like calcium sulfate or magnesium sulfate). The protein coagulates or curdles and is then pushed into a mold. The more water that is pushed out, the firmer the tofu. Tofu is much less flavorful than tempeh but does take on the flavors of whatever you cook it with. I use organic, non-GMO, extra-firm tofu to make savory dishes like tofu scramble or simply to slice and bake and add to stir-fries. Sprouted tofu is also a great choice if available. Tofu is found in the refrigerated

section in the health food aisle, usually near tempeh.

Pressing Tofu

Tofu is often "pressed" before used in recipes to remove water and improve the texture. To press tofu, simply drain the tofu, wrap it in a clean dish towel, and lay it on a level surface or in a colander and lay something heavy (three to five pounds) on top of the tofu and let it sit for about 20 minutes. Then, unwrap the tofu and it's ready to use. If you're in a hurry, I fully condone skipping pressing.

Silken tofu: This type of tofu is delicate and has the highest water content. It's coagulated, like firm tofu, but is not pressed. As its name indicates, it's silky and smooth. Silken tofu is available in soft, firm, and extra-firm but is usually reserved for blended, creamy desserts or dressings. You'll find silken tofu sealed in an aseptic, rectangular box often on the shelf (maybe fridge) in the organic or ethnic aisles. *Do not interchange regular tofu with silken tofu.*

Edamame: Edamame are immature, green soybeans. They have a mild flavor and are available still in their fuzzy, green pods or pre-shelled. You can find them fresh, but they're most often found in the freezer section of grocery stores. Edamame, like soybeans, provide complete protein but soybeans are more nutritionally dense (more calories, protein, fat, and carbs).

Pasta

I absolutely love pasta! I use pasta made from brown rice and quinoa as well as from lentils, green peas, and chickpeas! I keep a mix on hand at all times and always cook to al dente texture.

Nuts & Seeds

I use nuts and seeds in everything from baked goods to savory sauces and pantry seasonings. Each nut and seed has a different nutritional profile, flavor, and texture, and I like to incorporate them all! Almonds are my go-to. They're low in saturated fat and a great source of vitamin E. I use them for making milk and I'm borderline obsessed with almond butter (I prefer raw over roasted). Tahini (ground sesame seeds) is another favorite of mine. I use it as a base for a wide range of sauces, and it also provides calcium. Here are the nuts and seeds I used most often.

- Almonds
- Cashews
- Hazelnuts
- Pumpkin seeds
- Sesame seeds
- Sunflower seeds
- Walnuts

The Super Seeds

Hemp, chia, and flax seeds: These seeds are nutritional heavy lifters and deserve their own category. They're high on my list of must-include ingredients and are especially anti-inflammatory because of their concentration of essential fatty acids.

Hemp seeds: Hemp seeds (also known as hemp hearts) offer complete protein and a slew of important minerals like magnesium, iron, and zinc. They also offer a balanced package of omega-3 and omega-6 fats. Unlike chia and flax seeds, hemp seeds do not absorb liquid and can't be used as egg replacers or binders in recipes. They make great sauces, though! Creamy Hemp-Balsamic Dressing (recipe on page 107) is one of my go-to salad dressings!

Chia seeds: Chia seeds absorb a tremendous amount of liquid and are key to their namesake recipe, chia pudding! They're also a great source of complete protein, calcium, and omega-3 fats. They come in black and white varieties with black being the kind I use most often.

Flax seeds: Flax seeds are near and dear to my heart. They're a fabulous source of anti-inflammatory omega-3 fats, cancer-fighting lignans, and a boatload of fiber. Ground flax seeds (or flax meal) also has the ability to absorb water and is used often in baked goods as a thickener and egg replacer. I highly suggest making your own ground flax by grinding flax seeds in a coffee or spice grinder so it's as fresh as possible.

Herbs & Spices

Herbs and spices are flavor builders and essential components of any delicious dish. When paired with whole foods, they come together to make infinite flavor combinations, but they also offer surprising health benefits.

Fresh and dried herbs and spices provide powerful antioxidants and phytonutrients and can also keep sodium in check. When food falls flat or tastes bland, we usually reach for the saltshaker, whereas spices can elevate the flavor and reduce the need for salt! Note that dried spices are more concentrated in flavor than fresh, so if substituting fresh for dried, multiply the amount by three.

Storing Herbs

Keep dried herbs and spices in sealed bottles in a cool, dark, and dry place. I know we love to show off our spices in fancy spice racks on our kitchen counters but, unless used within a very short period of time, the spices will lose their flavor and also health benefits when exposed to light, oxygen, and heat.

Vinegars, Citrus & Seasonings

Vinegars and freshly squeezed citrus juices are fundamental ingredients that brighten and balance both sweet and savory meals. They're the first thing I turn to when I think a recipe is missing something. Here are the varieties you'll need for these recipes.

- Apple cider vinegar, raw, unfiltered and with the mother
- Balsamic vinegar (regular and white)
- Red and white wine vinegar
- Rice wine vinegar
- Lemon, lime, and orange juice and zest
- Tamari

Apple Cider Vinegar & "The Mother"

Apple cider vinegar is made from the fermentation of apple juice or apple cider. Unfiltered versions are unrefined, cloudy, and have some sediment settled at the bottom of the bottle. This sediment is "the mother" and is a collection or culture of bacteria responsible for turning apple cider into vinegar. These bacteria act like probiotics with a host of potential health benefits. The importance of including "the mother" is debated but I also prefer the taste of unfiltered apple cider and use this variety in my everyday cooking.

Tamari

Tamari is a gluten-free Japanese seasoning sauce made from fermented soybeans. It's used interchangeably with soy sauce (which is made with wheat) and gives food a savory, umami flavor. Tamari alternatives include coconut aminos (if you're looking for soy-free), liquid aminos, or soy sauce or shoyu (if gluten isn't an issue). If you're limiting sodium, you can also use reduced-sodium tamari instead of regular for any recipe throughout this book.

Canned/Bottled

I try to limit canned foods but when I do use them, I try my best to source BPA-free brands. Here are some canned and bottled goods I keep on hand.

- Tomato sauce and paste
- Whole, diced, and crushed tomatoes
- Capers or caper berries (in water or brine)
- Black and green olives (in water or brine)
- Roasted red peppers (packed in water)
- Pureed pumpkin

Sweeteners

Sugar is sugar is sugar. However, some sweeteners are better than others in that they have a lower glycemic index or provide additional nutrients. I've experimented with almost all the sweetener alternatives from yacon syrup to date crystals, and I've always come back to a handful of sweeteners because of their taste, functionality, availability, and health impact.

Many people choose to avoid sugar in all its forms, and I can get down with that! But I do think a little sweetener can go a long way in turning the healthiest plants into delicious culinary creations. (You could say I believe a little bit of sugar helps the medicine go down.) In small amounts and for occasional use, certain sweeteners work wonders! Here are some I use regularly.

Fresh fruit: Fruit is my favorite sweetener to use because we get the whole food and a lot of nutrients. I especially lean on ripe bananas, berries, apples, pureed pumpkin, and sweet potatoes to give texture and sweetness to desserts and baked goods.

Dried fruit: Dried fruits are more concentrated in sugar and less nutritious than fresh fruit but offer some vitamins, minerals, and fiber. I like to use raisins, mulberries, apricots, and goji berries but my favorite dried fruit for sweetening is dates. When dates are soaked in water they soften and are easy to blend with other ingredients. I like to use dates this way as sweeteners for sauces, piecrusts, and muffins. Medjool and Deglet Nour are my preferred dates and are widely available. Remember to remove and discard the pits!

Soaking Dates

Dates can have different textures from soft and juicy to dry and crumbly. For most recipes using dates, I suggest soaking them in hot water. The length of time to soak will depend on the dryness and freshness of your dates. Very fresh and soft Medjool dates, for example, often require no soaking at all!

Maple syrup: Maple syrup is the sap from maple trees boiled down into a dark liquid sugar. It's my preferred liquid sweetener for taste and it has some trace nutrients and antioxidants. Maple syrup is still high in sugar and should be used in limited amounts (even on pancakes!).

Coconut sugar: Coconut sugar is sugar from the sap of the coconut palm tree and is my preferred dry sweetener. It has a rich, caramel flavor, and I like to use it in baked goods and also in savory dishes (like my Sweet & Sour Chickpea-Stuffed Sweet Potatoes on page 183). Again, like maple syrup, coconut sugar is an improvement over refined white sugar, but it's still sugar and should be used sparingly or for special occasions.

Miscellaneous Ingredients

Nutritional yeast: This is a deactivated yeast that offers a cheesy taste to nut Parmesans (page 149), soups, and sauces. It's yellow in color and comes in flakes. This yeast is not the same as the yeast used to make bread or brew beer. Nutritional yeast has become a very popular ingredient, and you now can find this in most grocery stores. I consider it a must-have ingredient.

Chickpea flour: Or garbanzo bean flour, this is a flour made from chickpeas. It's very high in fiber and protein. It's my favorite flour to use for savory pancakes and mushroom omelets. Note that it tastes different (read: awful) when undercooked.

You can get this in most health food stores.

Dulse flakes: Dulse is a red seaweed. Seaweed is a phenomenal source of minerals, especially iodine, and I think it is an important addition to a plant-based diet. I, however, have never really taken to the texture of cooked seaweed, so I use dulse flakes to achieve a well-rounded nutritional profile in salads and grain dishes. The flavor is mild, and you can get this in health food stores.

Kombu: Kombu is a green seaweed. I use this for making vegetable broths and cooking legumes to help with digestion. After the broth and beans are cooked, I discard the kombu.

Salt

Excess sodium is bad for our health, that's as true as the sky is blue. However, if controlling your sodium intake is an important dietary consideration for you, limiting processed and packaged foods is key. Foods like commercial breads, frozen desserts, cheeses, and bottled sauces are a red flag for added salt. This might be as important if not more important than keeping the saltshaker off the dinner table.

Himalayan or Indian Black Salt (Kala Namak)

Not to be confused with pink Himalayan salt, this salt has a high sulfur content and smells just like eggs! It's an I-can't-believe-it's-not-eggs must-have ingredient for plant-based dishes like All-Day Tofu Scramble (recipe on page 55). You can get it in the ethnic grocery aisle, health food stores, and online. It comes in rock form and pre-ground; I prefer the ground version as it's easier to measure. This is a version of salt and a source of sodium, so keep this in mind if seasoning with additional salt.

If you're preparing the majority of your meals at home with whole foods (and you don't have a medical need to strictly limit your sodium), then adding quality salts when cooking is fine. I prefer to use sea salt and pink Himalayan salt in my kitchen. Pink Himalayan salt has more than 80 trace minerals! I keep a little bowl of salt on my counter for easy access and quick reseasoning prior to serving.

COOKING & PREPARATION METHODS

Basic Techniques

I didn't start cooking until I was in my twenties. And when I read a recipe instructing me to boil then simmer, or bake then broil, I wasn't exactly sure what the difference was. Here are some basic cooking techniques that you'll find throughout this book and a brief explanation.

Bake: Baking is a dry-heat method of cooking and is done by surrounding food with heat in the oven. Roasting is a similar cooking method but involves cooking at higher heat (400°F+).

Boil: Boiling food is cooking it by putting it in liquid that's rapidly boiling. Usually we bring liquid to a boil then reduce to a simmer for more even cooking.

Blend/process: I use a blender and food processor quite often. These tools literally make miracles happen when it comes to turning whole foods into creative and healthy meals. As mentioned before, it's definitely an investment, but a high-speed blender with a tamper is worth the money.

Steam: Steaming is cooking food by exposing it to the vapors of boiling liquid. Steaming is my favorite way to cook vegetables, as it preserves nutrients and is very convenient. I like to use an inexpensive steamer basket in a pot rather than a dedicated steamer pot. You simply put

the steamer basket in the pot, fill the pot with water (just below the steam basket), and bring to a boil. Once boiling, put the veggies in the basket, cover, and steam. Since steam is hotter than boiling water, vegetables, especially leafy greens, cook quickly.

Sauté: Sauté means to cook food rather quickly over medium-high heat. Traditional sauté is done with oil, but I skip the oil and instead use water or vegetable broth. A stir-fry method is similar but is usually done over high heat while stirring constantly.

Simmer: Simmering is cooking food by putting it in liquid that is gently boiling. This is how most soups are cooked. You can simmer food covered or uncovered, depending on the recipe.

Soak: Soaking is actually a very traditional cooking method! It's an important and easy step in some of my recipes. Soaking is straightforward—the food in question is put in a bowl and covered with water for a given amount of time. The soaking water is usually discarded, and the food is ready to use.

> ### Why Do We Soak?
> Soaking is a preparation method used to hydrate foods and also to neutralize certain compounds in foods that might inhibit nutrient absorption or availability. This is the main reason we soak legumes and grains–see how to cook legumes and grains on page 27. Soaking is also done to alter texture, cooking time, or flavor. In many of my recipes you'll see ingredients like nuts, dates, grains, and sun-dried tomatoes soaked and drained before being used.

Oil-Free Cooking

Oil-free cooking sounds like a technique that requires special skills, but it doesn't! It's painfully easy and will seriously change how you approach recipes. The secret to oil-free cooking is either to simply omit the oil or use a different ingredient instead.

First, oil-free sautéing or stir-frying is quite straightforward. I keep a large glass or measuring cup of water next to the stove and use it instead of oil and cook as per usual. Water for sautéing is not listed in the ingredient lists as the exact amount isn't important. As the water evaporates from the pan, I add more, a few tablespoons at a time, to prevent burning.

Baking without oil is also easy! Oils and butter are used generously in baked sweets like cakes, cookies, and pies. In this setting, fat and oils serve a few purposes—they create flaky texture, act as binders, and provide a certain taste and mouthfeel. I mostly use fruit purees and nut or seed butters to replace oils or butter in baked goods, and I dry-bake veggies, tofu, and beans, skipping the oil.

The other common use for oils is in sauces and salad dressings. Instead of oil, I use whole-food ingredients like veggies, nuts, seeds, or beans to thicken and add flavor and then I use water to thin if needed. You'll see that blending a range of ingredients from nuts to vegetables can create pourable, finger-licking sauces.

Cooking Grains

It might sound simple, but one of the most important skills I learned in culinary school was how to cook grains. Warm, fluffy grains are one of the most delicious dishes on the planet. Here's the simplest method for cooking delicious grains.

Cooking Grains

- The first step in making any grain is to rinse them under water in a fine-mesh colander. This removes any dirt or bitter plant compounds.
- Once rinsed and drained, transfer the grains to a small or medium-sized pot. Add the appropriate amount of water and salt (as instructed on the package).
- Cover the pot and bring the water to a boil. Once boiling, reduce to a simmer and simmer the grains, covered, for the directed amount of time. I cannot overstress how important it is to *not* remove the cover to check your grains while they're cooking, and never, ever stir your grains before they're completely cooked. I know that when I first started cooking grains, I found this process much easier to follow if I had pots with clear covers so I could see how the grains were cooking.
- Once the grains are cooked, turn the heat off and take the pot off the burner. Remove the cover and fluff the grains with a fork. Re-cover and let the grains sit for 5 to 10 minutes to continue steaming.

Other Grain Techniques

Soaking: Like legumes, grains can also be soaked overnight before cooking. This reduces the cooking time and water needed and also improves digestibility and availability of some nutrients in the grains. To soak, simply put the desired amount of grain in a bowl, cover with a couple of inches of water, and cover the bowl with a clean dishtowel. Let the grains soak overnight or for 6 to 8 hours. After the soaking time, drain the grains, rinse again, and then cook according to directions but add 25 percent less water than indicated. Note that the cooking time might also shorten by 5 to 10 minutes depending on the grain.

Toasting: To add more depth of flavor to your grains, you can try dry-toasting them before cooking. When you add the rinsed and drained grains to the pot, cook them on medium heat, stirring, for 1 to 2 minutes until you can smell the grain toasting. Then add water and continue cooking as you would normally.

Easy flavored grains: Sometimes I like to enhance my grains by spicing them up, literally. You can do this too by adding fresh or dried spices or herbs to your grains while they cook.

Cooking Legumes

Canned beans are convenient and are great in a pinch, but cooking beans from dried is more economical (canned are about 3 to 4 times more expensive than dried per serving), and allows you to control the ingredients added during cooking. If you've never cooked dried beans, make this a priority! You'll be surprised at how easy it is.

How to Cook Legumes

- Sort through the beans, discarding any pebbles, dirt, or oddly shaped ones.
- Place the beans in a large bowl, covering them with water by at least 4 inches (legumes will expand when soaked), and soak for 8 hours or overnight. Soaking improves the digestibility of beans and decreases cooking time. You do not need to soak smaller legumes like lentils or split peas (but this can still help shorten cooking time).
- After soaking, discard the soaking water and rinse the beans. If you don't have time to cook them after they've been soaked, simply change the water and place them in the fridge. You can leave them

in the fridge soaking for up to 2 days. Just change the water every 10 to 12 hours.

- Place the rinsed beans in a pot, covering them with at least 2 to 3 inches of water. Optional: Add a 3-inch piece of kombu (to help with digestibility).
- Cover the pot and bring to a boil. Once boiling, reduce to a simmer and cook partially covered. Cooking time varies but is usually between 1 and 1½ hours. Keep checking in to make sure the water hasn't evaporated. Toward the end you can add a pinch or two of salt if desired.
- The beans are done when you can squish one between your fingers (not falling apart but no longer hard in the middle). Once they're fully cooked, take the pot to the kitchen sink and drain the beans in a colander. I like to save the cooking liquid and store any unused beans in this liquid in the fridge. *This cooking liquid is also known as aquafaba.* You can also use the cooking liquid in soups or stews. If you used kombu, discard or compost.

- If you prefer using canned beans, I suggest choosing organic brands with no added salt or sugar and a brand that does not use BPA in their can lining (like Eden Foods).

Tips for Cooking Beans
- Beans expand once soaked and cooked. One cup of dried beans will become 1½–2 ½ cups cooked (depending on the bean).
- Foam will develop on top of beans when they first start boiling; simply skim it off and discard.
- Be sure to use appropriately sized pots to reduce the risk of boiling over.
- Keep cooking water at a gentle simmer and not a rapid boil. Cooking in boiling water for long periods of time will likely overcook the beans and increase the risk of their splitting/falling apart.
- Avoid cooking different kinds of beans at the same time. Different beans have various cooking times.
- While cooking, ensure the beans are always covered by water and stir occasionally to prevent sticking.
- Use a pressure cooker to reduce cooking time.

TIPS, TRICKS & SHORTCUTS

Truth: There is no substitute for home cooking. Preparing your own food takes time, but it doesn't have to take *all* your time, and there are things you can do to simplify plant-based food prep. Here a few things I keep in mind and that I regularly share with others on how to make meal planning easier and healthier.

Make grains and beans in batches. When you have cooked grains and legumes on hand, meal prep can be much easier. I like to batch cook a grain and bean every three days or so. I cook them according to directions, wait for them to cool, and then refrigerate them in a sealed container.

Sauce! I believe sauces are the holy-grail secret ingredient to a produce-packed, easy, and delicious plant-based diet. I recommend having a sauce or two on hand at all times to use as a salad dressing, bowl sauce, or to smother over baked potatoes and steamed greens. I use a variety of sauces made from whole foods consistently throughout this book. I suggest getting familiar with a

couple so you can whip them up from memory.

Freeze foods. Having healthy meals and snacks frozen and ready for defrosting is, as they say, *everything*. And I have found that you can freeze almost *anything*. Here's what I suggest keeping in the deep freezer to avoid hunger emergencies when time is short:

- *Muffins*: Keep a batch of muffins in the freezer at all times for on-the-go breakfasts or snacks.
- *Soups*: I like to have a few servings of two different soups in the freezer. Take them out the night before and let them thaw on the kitchen counter or in the fridge and enjoy for lunch or recycle for dinner.
- *Bean burgers and balls*: The payoff of having bean burgers and bean balls cooked and kept in the freezer cannot be overstated. I like to crumble burgers into my salad (like the Loaded Lunch Salad on

page 107) or mix and match a burger or falafel recipe with a combination of raw or steamed veggies and a sauce (like the Golden Bowls on page 169).

- *Sweets*: You'll see in the Sweets & Treats chapter (page 211) that some of my preferred sweets can be eaten right from the freezer or require a short defrosting time. I always keep at least one batch of bliss balls in the freezer as well as a presliced cake!

Make dinner . . . and lunch. I've found that preparing lunch while making dinner is the easiest way to prepare multiple meals. Either make extra dinner and use leftovers as lunch, or actually make lunch while you're making dinner. That way you don't have to clean up twice.

Chop first. Veggie-forward recipes often move fast and come together quickly, but you have to be ready. If you're new to preparing produce-based meals, I suggest chopping and prepping all the veggies before starting in on a recipe.

Season last. I like to add salt or sodium-rich seasonings at the end of my recipes. This way you can avoid oversalting. Taste and reseason until you get it how you like it.

PART II
RECIPES

Notes for All Recipes

- You can always substitute low-sodium tamari for regular.
- Use freshly squeezed citrus when orange, lemon, or lime juice is called for.
- When using apple cider vinegar, use raw, unfiltered, with "the mother" varieties.
- Stir all your nut and seed butters before adding to a recipe.
- "Dry" grains or beans means uncooked.
- When salt is called for, you can use pink Himalayan salt or sea salt and finish each recipe with a taste test and reseason if needed.
- For recipes that call for several different dried spices, measure the spices into a small bowl before starting to cook. This saves times and keeps the "add spices" step quick and easy.
- Adjust spicy seasonings like red pepper flakes and cayenne pepper to your liking.
- Read a recipe in its entirety before cooking so you know if any soaking, pressing, or additional preparations are required.

BREAKFAST BOWLS, BLENDS & BRUNCH

THE KIND WORTH WAKING UP FOR

I'm an early bird! I like to start the day with a big glass of room-temperature water (sometimes with a squeeze of lemon) and a little mindfulness (yoga, meditation, and, yes, coffee!). Then I'm ready for something wholesome and nutritious.

I lean more toward fruit, grain, and blended breakfasts. I like my first meal of the day to be fresh and filling but not heavy and not too sweet—the Sunshine Smoothie (page 42) or Everyday Overnight Oats (page 37) are in my regular rotation.

If you appreciate a savory start to the day, I've included some of my favorites as well (who can live without tofu scramble?).

I hope you find a few quick favorites and lazy brunch must-haves in the following pages!

Everyday Overnight Oats 37

Rise n' Shine Smoothie Bowl 38

Raw Green Buckwheat Bowl 41

Sunshine Smoothie 42

Butterm*lk Buckwheat Pancakes with Almond Butter Caramel 45

Cinnamon-Spiced House Granola 48

Cozy Pumpkin Bowls 51

Layered Berry Chia Pudding & Creamy Oat Parfait 52

All-Day Tofu Scramble 55

Chickpea & Avocado Savory Pancakes 56

Everyday Overnight Oats

This is an overnight oats/chia pudding hybrid that takes only minutes to assemble. All the work is done in the fridge while you sleep. If I have time, I jazz it up like you see in the pictures, but otherwise I put it in a mason jar and go! Berries give a nice pop of color, sweetness, and nutrition.

Makes 3–4 servings

Ingredients

1½ cups gluten-free old-fashioned rolled oats

3 tablespoons chia seeds

1 cup blueberries or raspberries, fresh or frozen*

¾ teaspoon cinnamon

2 cups unsweetened almond milk or organic soy milk

¼ teaspoon pure vanilla extract

1–2 tablespoons maple syrup, optional

Optional Toppings

Fruit of choice

Cinnamon-Spiced House Granola (page 48)

Drizzle of nut butter or Almond Butter Caramel (page 45)

Preparation

1. Add the oats, chia seeds, berries, and cinnamon to a large container with a lid. Add the milk, vanilla, and maple syrup (if using). Stir, cover, and keep in the fridge overnight.

2. In the morning stir, add more milk if desired, divide among bowls, and garnish with optional toppings. If you prefer warm oats, you can warm a portion on the stove over low heat.

Nutritional Nugget

Oats are extremely nutritious! They provide a host of essential minerals like iron and zinc as well as protein and important soluble fiber that helps balance blood sugar, reduce cholesterol, and keep you full for hours.

---

* As frozen berries thaw, they'll change the color of the milk.

Rise n' Shine Smoothie Bowl

Smoothie bowls are like thick versions of smoothies you eat with a spoon (instead of a straw). I love smoothie bowls because they take longer to eat, encourage chewing (which helps with digestion), and allow for all kinds of nutrient-rich toppings! When I first started sharing recipes on RiseShineCook.ca, smoothie bowls had just hit the health food scene. I took every opportunity to experiment and this combination was one that stuck. You can turn this into a smoothie by adding more milk.

Makes 2 servings

Ingredients

½ cup unsweetened almond milk

1 large frozen banana

1 heaping cup frozen mango or mixed berries

1 cup packed baby spinach

1 tablespoon hemp seeds

1 tablespoon whole flax seeds

1 tablespoon well-stirred almond butter

Pinch cinnamon

Optional Toppings

¼ cup Cinnamon-Spiced House Granola (page 48)

Chia seeds, goji berries, fresh berries, shredded
  coconut

Preparation

1. Add all the smoothie ingredients to a blender in the order listed. Blend on high until smooth, using your tamper to assist with the blending. For a thinner consistency, add more milk. For a thicker smoothie, reduce the milk.

2. Divide the smoothie between bowls and garnish as you wish!

Raw Green Buckwheat Bowl

This breakfast bowl is made by soaking whole buckwheat groats overnight and then blending them with banana and almond milk. I like to add leafy greens for extra phytonutrients—you can't even taste them! Soaking softens the groats, makes them easier to digest, and activates key nutrients. For a lighter or nut-free version, omit the almond butter. These are small servings but very filling!

Makes 3 servings

Ingredients

1 cup raw buckwheat groats, soaked overnight

¾ cup unsweetened almond or organic soy milk (plus more if needed)

1 medium, ripe banana

1–2 tablespoons maple syrup or 2–3 pitted soft Medjool dates, optional

1 cup baby spinach

1 tablespoon ground flax seeds

1 tablespoon well-stirred almond butter

Pinch cinnamon

Optional Toppings
Fresh berries
Sliced banana

Preparation

1. Place the buckwheat in a medium-sized bowl, cover with a few inches of water, and lay a clean dishcloth over the bowl. Soak overnight on the counter or in the fridge.

2. In the morning, drain the buckwheat in a fine-mesh strainer and rinse well. The liquid that drains off will be thick and goopy and will take a few minutes to drain off—this is normal. Set the buckwheat aside and discard the drained liquid.

3. Place the almond milk, banana, maple syrup or drained dates, spinach, flax seeds, almond butter, and cinnamon in a blender and blend until smooth.

4. Now, add the drained buckwheat and blend again. I like to leave a little texture, but feel free to blend until smooth. Add more milk as needed to reach your desired consistency. Divide among bowls and garnish with berries and sliced banana.

Variations: This is a flexible recipe. Add more or less almond butter, greens, or sweetener to your liking. If you really like it green, swap the spinach for kale!

Sunshine Smoothie

I wanted to make a chameleon smoothie that was wonderfully nutritious and beautiful with or without greens! Turmeric and ginger offer complementary inflammation-fighting compounds, pineapple provides digestive enzymes, and flax and hemp seeds deliver essential fatty acids. This is something to wake up for and feel good about! Make it blue and equally healthy by swapping pineapple for frozen blueberries.

Makes 2 servings

Ingredients

1 cup unsweetened almond milk or water (plus more if needed)

¼ teaspoon ground turmeric

¼–½ inch knob of ginger, depending on preference

1 tablespoon ground flax seeds

1 tablespoon hemp seeds

1½ cups frozen pineapple or blueberries (or half and half)

1 large frozen banana

Pinch cinnamon

Green Option:

1 packed cup spinach or kale

Preparation

1. Add all ingredients to a blender in the order listed. Blend on high and add more milk as needed while blending to achieve your preferred consistency.

Nutritional Nuggets

- Smoothies are convenient and delicious but it's easy to make them high in sugar and/or calories. Try limiting fruit to 1 to 1½ cups per serving and avoid adding extra sugars in the form of syrups or powders.

- Drinking your smoothie quickly (I'm guilty!) can cause digestive issues, low energy, or hunger. Try chewing a little when you drink your smoothie (this activates digestive enzymes) and sip slowly.

- Finally, if you find that you're hungry again soon after having a smoothie for breakfast, try a more solid breakfast (like overnight oats) to see if this keeps you full longer.

Butterm*lk Buckwheat Pancakes with Almond Butter Caramel

Pancakes—not just a vehicle for a syrup! These pancakes are nutritiously made with whole-grain buckwheat and brown rice flour, banana, and chia seeds. They're satisfying and, when served with date-sweetened Almond Butter Caramel, pretty much addictive! The batter is sugar-free, so I suggest adjusting sweetener to taste in the form of fresh fruit or a drizzle of maple syrup once plated.

Makes 8–10 pancakes

Ingredients

Almond Butter Caramel

6 pitted Medjool dates, soaked in hot water for 15–30 minutes

½ cup well-stirred almond butter

¼ teaspoon cinnamon

¼ teaspoon sea salt

¾ cup unsweetened almond milk or organic soy milk

*Butterm*lk Pancakes*

1¾ cups unsweetened almond milk or organic soy milk

1 tablespoon freshly squeezed lemon juice or apple cider vinegar

1 cup buckwheat flour

½ cup brown rice flour

1 tablespoon arrowroot starch

1 tablespoon baking powder

1¼ teaspoons cinnamon

¼ teaspoon sea salt

1 medium, ripe banana

1 tablespoon chia seeds

½ teaspoon pure vanilla extract

Fresh fruit of choice, for serving

Preparation

1. First, make the almond caramel (if using). Drain the dates, discard the soaking water, and add the dates, almond butter, cinnamon, salt, and almond milk to a high-speed blender and blend on high until smooth. Add more almond milk if needed, 1 tablespoon at a time, to reach desired consistency. Transfer to a jar or bowl and set aside.

2. Now, make the pancakes. Preheat the oven to its lowest temperature (around 200°F) and line a baking pan with parchment paper and place in the oven.

3. In a medium bowl, mix the almond milk with the lemon juice or apple cider vinegar and set aside for 5 minutes to create butterm*lk.

4. Add the buckwheat flour, brown rice flour, arrowroot, baking powder, cinnamon, and salt to a large bowl and mix to combine.

5. Add the butterm*lk (almond milk/lemon juice or apple cider vinegar mixture) to a blender along with banana, chia seeds, and vanilla and blend until smooth. Add the blended mixture to the dry ingredients and mix together with a whisk until no lumps or

(Continued on next page)

dry spots remain. The batter should be thick but pourable.

6. Warm a nonstick pan over medium heat. Once the pan is hot, scoop out ⅓ to ½ cup of batter and pour onto the pan. Shake the pan a little if needed to spread the pancake. Cook for 2 to 4 minutes or until bubbles form all across the top of the pancake and the edges are dry. Flip and cook for another minute. Transfer the cooked pancakes to the baking sheet (in a single layer) in the oven to keep warm. Repeat with remaining batter. Remember that after the first batch, the pan will be hotter and the cooking time for the remaining pancakes will shorten.

7. Serve the pancakes with fresh fruit and Almond Butter Caramel. Leftover sauce can be kept in the fridge for up to 5 days and added to overnight oats, drizzled on Easy Apple-Berry Crumble (recipe on page 213) or used as a fruit dip.

Variations: When making the almond caramel, you can use ¼ cup maple syrup instead of dates and reduce the milk to ¼ cup. Add more milk as you blend to reach a pourable consistency.

Cinnamon-Spiced House Granola

A healthy, oil-free granola (that's also affordable) is often hard to find—believe me, I've looked everywhere! Fortunately, it's so easy to make your own. This is a lightly sweetened, loose granola baked on low heat that I always have on hand to add to smoothie bowls and chia puddings or to have as a snack. Remember that granola won't be crunchy when it's first removed from the oven but will harden as it cools.

Makes 4 cups

Ingredients

3 cups gluten-free old-fashioned rolled oats
1 cup sliced almonds
1 tablespoon cinnamon
½ teaspoon ground allspice
½ teaspoon sea salt
½ cup maple syrup
¼ cup unsweetened applesauce
1 tablespoon pure vanilla extract
¼ cup water

Optional Additions
1½ cups dried fruit of choice, extra seeds, nuts, or cacao nibs

---

Almond Milk

Homemade nut milks put commercial varieties to shame! Here's how I do it.

- Soak 1 cup of almonds overnight.

- Drain in the morning, add the almonds to a blender with 4 cups of water, a big pinch of salt, and 2 teaspoons of vanilla extract.

- Blend on high for 1 minute. Strain the milk through a nut milk bag and you're done! Keep almond milk in the fridge for up to 4 days.

Variations: Use pumpkin or sunflower seeds instead of almonds for a nut-free version.

Preparation

1. Position the oven rack in the middle of the oven and preheat to 300°F. Line a large baking sheet with parchment paper.

2. In a large bowl, mix the oats, almonds, cinnamon, allspice, and salt.

3. In a separate small bowl, whisk together the maple syrup, applesauce, vanilla, and water.

4. Add the wet ingredients to the dry and mix well with a spatula until no dry spots remain. Transfer the mixture to the baking pan and spread the mixture on the pan into a single layer, making sure there are no clumps of oats.

5. Bake for 65 to 70 minutes, flipping every 15 minutes for even cooking. The granola is done when it's browned and feels completely dry to the touch, with no soft or damp spots. Note that it won't feel crunchy yet but will crunch up as it cools. Remove from the oven and let the granola cool completely on the pan before putting it in a sealed container.

6. If you want more texture or an extra hit of sweetness, mix the granola with 1½ cup of dried fruit like raisins, chopped apricots, or cranberries. You can also add extra seeds, nuts, or cacao nibs! Keep the granola in a cool, dry place for up to a month.

Cozy Pumpkin Bowls

Even if you don't like pumpkin, you've got to try this bowl! It's creamy yet light and has a blissful combination of warm spices and sweet notes from dates and orange juice. Pumpkin is filling, rich in fiber, and a fantastic source of beta-carotene (a precursor to vitamin A and crucial antioxidant). Use leftover pumpkin puree to make Pumpkin Pie Squares (page 217).

Makes 2 servings

Ingredients

2–4 pitted Medjool dates, soaked in hot water for 15–30 minutes

¾ cup unsweetened almond milk (plus more if needed)

⅓ cup gluten-free old-fashioned rolled oats

⅓ cup unsweetened pumpkin puree

2 tablespoons freshly squeezed orange juice

1 tablespoon + 2 teaspoons well-stirred almond butter

½ teaspoon cinnamon

¼ teaspoon ground nutmeg

¼ teaspoon ground turmeric

Pinch sea salt

Toppings:
Blueberries, chia seeds, Cinnamon-Spiced House Granola (page 48) or preferred granola

Preparation

1. Drain the dates, discard the soaking liquid, and add dates and all other ingredients (except toppings) to a high-speed blender. Blend on high until completely smooth, adding more milk, 1 to 2 tablespoons at a time, to thin the mix if desired.

2. Divide the blended mix between 2 bowls and top with berries, chia seeds, and granola.

Layered Berry Chia Pudding & Creamy Oat Parfait

An immediate mood booster! Serve these pretty parfaits for brunch or take a jar for breakfast on the go. There are two layers—berry chia pudding and creamy nut butter overnight oats. Make them both separately in a blender, refrigerate overnight, and then layer in the morning.

Makes 4–6 servings

Ingredients

Berry Chia Pudding

2 cups unsweetened organic soy or homemade
  Almond Milk (page 48)*

1 cup mixed frozen berries (raspberries,
  blackberries, and blueberries are ideal)

2 tablespoons maple syrup, optional

¼ teaspoon cinnamon

½ cup chia seeds

Creamy Oats

2 cups unsweetened almond or organic soy milk

1 medium, ripe banana

¼ cup nut butter of choice (I prefer almond butter)

¼ teaspoon cinnamon

½ teaspoon pure vanilla extract

Pinch sea salt

2 cups gluten-free old-fashioned rolled oats

1 tablespoon ground flax seeds

Garnish

Berries, chopped nuts, sliced banana

Preparation

1. First, make the chia pudding. Add all the chia pudding ingredients, except chia seeds, to a high-speed blender and blend until smooth. Transfer the mix to a large container with a lid and stir in the chia seeds. Secure the lid and shake the container for a few seconds. Shake every few minutes for 15 minutes (this prevents the chia seeds from clumping together) and then refrigerate overnight.

2. Next, make the oats. Rinse the blender container and then add all the ingredients, except oats and flax seeds, to the blender and blend until smooth. Transfer this mix to a separate container, stir in the oats and flax seeds, cover, and refrigerate overnight.

3. In the morning, layer ½ to ¾ cup each of the berry chia pudding and creamy oats in bowls or jars and garnish as you wish.

*Commercial almond milk is usually too thin to create a creamy chia pudding. Soy milk or homemade nut milks, generally thicker, will deliver better results.

All-Day Tofu Scramble

Don't let the long list here intimidate you, it's mostly spices! After making every version of tofu scramble I've come across, this method, where the tofu is marinated, is by far my favorite! I suggest first pressing and marinating the tofu and then moving onto the roasted potatoes and sautéed veggies. You can serve this as a layered dish, as in the picture, or serve the scramble and potatoes separately.

Makes 3 servings

Ingredients

Tofu Scramble Marinade

1 tablespoon nutritional yeast

½ teaspoon ground cumin

½ teaspoon garlic powder

¼ teaspoon red pepper flakes

¼ teaspoon onion powder

¼ teaspoon ground turmeric

¼ teaspoon dried oregano

3 grinds black pepper

½ teaspoon Indian black salt (kala namak) or sea salt

1 tablespoon freshly squeezed lemon juice

1 teaspoon Dijon mustard

2 tablespoons water

1 (12–14 ounce) package extra-firm organic tofu, pressed (see page 17 for pressing instructions)

Potatoes and Veggies

3 medium Yukon Gold potatoes, peel left on, chopped into ¾-inch cubes

1 medium red or yellow onion, diced

½ red bell pepper, diced

4 ounces button mushrooms, quartered or chopped

1 cup loosely packed chopped kale or baby spinach

1 avocado, pit removed, peeled, and thinly sliced

Optional Additions

Salsa, cherry tomatoes, hot sauce, cilantro

Preparation

1. First, marinate the tofu. Mix the nutritional yeast, all the spices, black salt, lemon juice, Dijon, and water into a loose paste in a medium-sized bowl. After the tofu is pressed, crumble it into the bowl with the marinade. Mix well and let the tofu sit in the marinade while preparing the potatoes.

2. Preheat the oven to 425°F and line a baking sheet with parchment paper. Spread the diced potatoes out on the pan and season with salt and pepper. Bake for 30 to 35 minutes, flipping halfway through, or until tender and easily pierced with a fork.

3. After you've flipped the potatoes, start the scramble. In a large, nonstick sauté pan, sauté the onion with a few tablespoons of water for 5 minutes. Now, add the red pepper and mushrooms and continue to cook for another 5 minutes, stirring often, until the mushrooms shrink in size.

4. Next, add the marinated tofu (and any leftover marinade) to the pan and cook on medium heat for another 5 to 6 minutes, again stirring often. Mix in the greens and remove from heat. Here you can add the roasted potatoes to the pan and mix together or plate alongside the scramble and top with sliced avocado, salsa, tomatoes, and a pinch of salt. Serve with hot sauce and cilantro if desired.

Chickpea & Avocado Savory Pancakes

This recipe was inspired by my favorite avocado toast combo but, instead of bread, we're using savory pancakes made from chickpea flour. Our House Hummus (page 132) is my preferred topping but feel free to use any hummus you like! I like to pair this with a simple side salad.

Makes 8–10 pancakes

Ingredients

Savory Pancakes

1½ cups chickpea (garbanzo bean) flour

3 tablespoons nutritional yeast

1½ teaspoons baking powder

1½ teaspoons garlic powder

1 teaspoon onion powder

½ teaspoon ground turmeric

¼ teaspoon red pepper flakes or to your preference

¼ teaspoon sea salt

2 pinches black pepper

1⅓ cup unsweetened almond milk or water

2 tablespoons freshly squeezed lemon juice

¾ cup finely chopped spinach, optional

Toppings

1 cup Our House Hummus (page 132)

1 ripe avocado, pit removed, peeled, and thinly sliced

2 cups cherry tomatoes, quartered

½ English cucumber, thinly sliced

Preparation

1. Preheat the oven to its lowest temperature (around 200°F) and line a baking sheet with parchment paper and place in the oven.

2. Add all the pancake ingredients (except spinach) to a medium-sized bowl. Whisk until the batter is smooth, then stir in the spinach (if using).

3. Warm a nonstick pan over medium heat. Once the pan is hot, scoop out ⅓ cup batter for each pancake and pour onto the pan. Cook for 2 to 4 minutes or until bubbles form across the top of the pancakes and the edges are dry. Flip and cook for another minute. Transfer the cooked pancakes to the oven to keep warm.

4. Repeat with remaining batter. Remember that after the first batch the pan will be hotter and the cooking time for the pancakes will shorten.

5. Plate the pancakes and top with a dollop of hummus, sliced avocado, cherry tomatoes, and cucumber.

Variations: Skip the hummus and avocado and serve these pancakes with Golden Tahini Sauce (page 169) and top them with roasted or sautéed veggies.

THE BREAKFAST BAKERY
BETTER BAKED GOODS

These baked goods are ideal for the morning hours and also great as snacks. For years I searched for baked goods that were made with whole foods rather than white flours, sugars, or processed oils. Gluten-free baked goods were particularly awful.

I finally realized that I was going to have to get creative and make them myself.

In this chapter you'll find inventive ways of making traditional favorites like breads, bagels, and muffins.

There are a few key ingredients and a couple of techniques that I've found to be essential in making tasty, textured, and healthy baked goods. It's helpful to review the Baking Notes (page 60).

You can feel good about these baked goods.

Apricot, Cardamom & Blueberry Bars   63

Apple, Almond & Chickpea Muffins   64

Cranberry-Orange Muffins with Rosemary   67

Amazing Multigrain Bread   69

Blueberry, Banana & Chia Muffins   72

Mini Buckwheat Bagels   75

Banana-Raspberry Breakfast Bake Casserole   76

Baking Notes

Measure Ingredients Exactly

Unlike savory recipes, most baking recipes require exact measurements. I recommend using measuring cups and spoons and never eyeballing things like flours, baking sodas, powders, or starches. Use the straight edge of a butter knife to level measuring cups.

Lining Baking Pans

Essential in preventing cakes and baked goods from sticking to pans is parchment paper. I line square and rectangle baking dishes so that the paper hangs out over two opposing sides. This allows you to pull whatever you're making out of the pan easily. For circular cake and springform pans, I trace the bottom of the pan onto parchment paper and cut it out, so it fits perfectly. You don't need to line silicone pans.

Silicone Pans

Silicone baking pans are a fantastic tool for healthy baking. I use my 3-inch donut pans and Bundt pans most often and alternate between silicone and traditional muffin pans. Note that baking times in silicone baking pans are usually longer.

Cooking Times

Oven temperatures vary, but once you get a sense of your oven, you'll be able to navigate the recommended baking times. Follow the recipe as written, but if it seems like your version is baking faster or slower, let the baked good guide you and adjust as needed.

Cooling

Most baked goods require cooling in the pan and then on a cooling rack. This allows the baked good to set as baking still continues even when it's removed from the oven. Avoid cutting off a slice or sneaking a bite until the cooling time is up (I know, the temptation is real).

Sweeteners

I like to use a combination of whole foods, citrus, and minimally processed sweeteners to make my baked goods. From whole dates to bananas and maple syrup to coconut sugar. Feel free to adjust added sweeteners to your liking.

Apricot, Cardamom & Blueberry Bars

Fragrant, wholesome, and nutritious, these breakfast bars are dense and filling. They're lightly sweetened and scattered with nuts, seeds, and dried fruit. Cardamom is the distinctive spice that gives these bars depth of flavor.

Makes 9 squares

Ingredients

1 tablespoon whole psyllium husk

½ cup water

1 cup gluten-free old-fashioned rolled oats

1 cup quinoa flakes

¾ cup gluten-free oat flour

½ cup coconut sugar

½ cup walnuts, chopped

¾ cup dried apricots, finely chopped

3 tablespoons hemp seeds or sesame seeds

1 teaspoon cinnamon

1¼ teaspoons ground cardamom

¼ teaspoon sea salt

⅔ cup unsweetened almond milk

1 tablespoon pure vanilla extract

Zest from 1 large orange (1 heaping tablespoon)

2 tablespoons freshly squeezed orange juice

1 cup fresh or frozen blueberries

Nutritional Nugget

Quinoa flakes are whole quinoa rolled into flakes. They're a good source of protein and fiber and give baked goods a unique texture. You can find quinoa flakes in health food stores and online.

Variations: For a nut-free version, use soy milk instead of almond milk and pumpkin seeds instead of walnuts.

Preparation

1. Position the oven rack in the middle of the oven and preheat to 350°F. Line an 8 x 8 inch baking pan with parchment paper so that the parchment paper hangs out over two opposing sides.

2. In a small bowl, mix the psyllium husk with ½ cup of water and set aside for 5 minutes to thicken.

3. In a large bowl, mix together the rolled oats, quinoa flakes, oat flour, coconut sugar, walnuts, apricots, hemp seeds, cinnamon, cardamom, and salt.

4. Now, add the almond milk, vanilla, orange zest and juice, and psyllium/water mix to the bowl and mix with a spatula until no dry spots remain. Fold in the blueberries.

5. Transfer the mix to the parchment-paper-lined pan and spread it evenly with a spatula.

6. Bake for 23 to 26 minutes or until the surface is firm to the touch and lightly browned along the edges. Remove from the oven and let cool for 15 minutes in the pan on a cooling rack. Then, remove the squares from the pan by pulling on the overhanging parchment paper.

7. Let cool completely on a cooling rack before cutting into 9 squares using a sharp chef's knife (not a serrated knife). These will keep in the fridge for 4 days or in the freezer for up to 3 months.

Apple, Almond & Chickpea Muffins

Muffin batter made from chickpeas—literally, a culinary jaw-drop moment for me! These delicious muffin miracles are low in sugar and full of protein and fiber! I like to use my 3¼ ounce spring-release scoop or disher (loosely packed with batter) to scoop the batter into the muffin tin—it creates a clean, nicely shaped muffin.

Makes 10 muffins

Ingredients

1½ cups gluten-free oat flour

½ cup gluten-free old-fashioned rolled oats

¼ cup coconut sugar

3 tablespoons hemp seeds

2 teaspoons baking powder

½ teaspoon baking soda

1¼ teaspoons cinnamon

½ teaspoon ground allspice

¼ teaspoon sea salt

½ cup unsweetened almond milk

1 cup cooked or canned chickpeas, drained and rinsed

⅓ cup unsweetened applesauce

⅓ cup well-stirred almond butter

2 tablespoons maple syrup

1 teaspoon pure vanilla extract

⅓ cup raisins

1 medium apple, peel on or off, diced

Garnish

Thinly sliced apple

Variations: For a nut-free version, use sunflower seed butter instead of almond butter and soy milk instead of almond milk.

Preparation

1. Position the oven rack in the middle of the oven and preheat to 350°F.
2. In a large bowl, mix together oat flour, rolled oats, coconut sugar, hemp seeds, baking powder, baking soda, cinnamon, allspice, and salt. Break up any chunks of coconut sugar and set the bowl aside.
3. Add the almond milk, chickpeas, applesauce, almond butter, maple syrup, and vanilla to a blender and blend until smooth.
4. Add the blended mix to the dry ingredients and mix until combined. Fold in the raisins and chopped apple.
5. Scoop a heaping ⅓ cup of the batter for each muffin, again I use a spring-release scoop or disher. You have the option to garnish the muffins with thinly sliced apple, pressed lightly into the batter. Bake the muffins for 18 to 20 minutes or until slightly firm to the touch and golden in color.
6. Remove the muffins from the oven, place on a cooling rack, and let them cool in the muffin tin for 15 minutes. If using a nonstick or traditional muffin tin, use a thin spatula to run along the edge of each muffin and pop them out. If using a silicone muffin pan, let the muffins cool until the pan is no longer hot, then pull the sides of the pan to release the muffins. Place the muffins on the cooling rack and let them cool completely. Keep these muffins in the fridge for 3 days or in the freezer for up to 3 months.

Cranberry-Orange Muffins with Rosemary

This is a classic muffin (my mom's favorite), just reinvented. Cranberries are rich in phytonutrients and are lower in sugar than most fruit but are generally passed over for other berries. Here, their tartness combines with oats, orange juice, and tahini to make a delicious low-sugar muffin. For an extra special touch and a little hint of elegance, add fresh chopped rosemary!

Makes 12 muffins

Ingredients

2 teaspoons whole psyllium husk

⅓ cup water

¾ cup blanched almond flour

1¾ cup gluten-free oat flour

1¾ cups gluten-free old-fashioned rolled oats

1 tablespoon baking powder

¾ teaspoon cinnamon

Heaping ¼ teaspoon ground nutmeg

¾ teaspoon sea salt

Scant ½ cup unsweetened almond milk

⅓ cup unsweetened applesauce

Zest of 1 large orange (1 heaping tablespoon)

⅓ cup freshly squeezed orange juice

3 tablespoons well-stirred tahini

⅓ cup maple syrup

1½ teaspoons pure vanilla extract

1½ cups frozen or fresh cranberries

3 tablespoons finely chopped fresh rosemary leaves

Preparation

1. Position the oven rack in the middle of the oven and preheat to 350°F.

2. In a small bowl, mix together the psyllium husk and ⅓ cup water. Set aside for 5 minutes to thicken.

3. Add the almond flour, oat flour, oats, baking powder, cinnamon, nutmeg, and salt to a medium-sized bowl and mix, breaking up any chunks of almond flour.

4. Add the almond milk, applesauce, orange zest and juice, tahini, maple syrup, vanilla, and the thickened psyllium mix to a blender and blend until smooth.

5. Add the blended mixture to the bowl of dry ingredients and mix using a spatula until no dry spots remain. Fold in the cranberries and rosemary.

6. Scoop a heaping ⅓ cup of the batter, I like to use my 3¼ ounce spring-release scoop or disher, for each muffin and bake the muffins for 23 to 26 minutes or until the muffins are almost firm to the touch.

7. Remove the muffins from the oven, place on a cooling rack, and let them cool in the muffin tin for 15 minutes. If using a nonstick or traditional muffin tin, use a thin spatula to run along the edge of each muffin and

(Continued on next page)

pop them out. If using a silicone muffin pan, let the muffins cool until the pan is no longer hot, then pull the sides of the pan to release the muffins. Place the muffins on the cooling rack and let them cool completely. The bottoms of the muffins might seem damp, but they will dry and firm as they cool. Keep these muffins in the fridge for 2 to 3 days or in the freezer for up to 3 months.

Variations: For a nut-free version, swap another ¾ cup of oat flour for the almond flour and soy milk for almond milk.

Amazing Multigrain Bread

This bread is the ideal whole-food breakfast bread! It's made from whole quinoa, buckwheat, and rolled oats! No flour, no yeast, and takes about ten minutes of actual work. I like it best double toasted and smothered in raw almond butter with a sprinkle of sea salt! My first version of this bread, years ago, was inspired by my all-time favorite whole-food chef, Amy Chaplin. If you don't already have them, go buy her incredible cookbooks!

Makes 1 loaf or 12–14 slices

Ingredients

½ cup dry white quinoa

¾ cup raw buckwheat groats

¼ cup whole psyllium husk

1½ cups water

2 cups gluten-free old-fashioned rolled oats, divided

1 tablespoon + 1 teaspoon baking powder

2 tablespoons apple cider vinegar

1½ teaspoons sea salt

¼ cup chia seeds

¼ cup hemp seeds

Preparation

1. Add the quinoa and buckwheat to a large bowl and cover with 3 inches of water. Cover the bowl with a clean dishcloth and let the grains soak overnight on the counter, or for 6 to 8 hours.

2. After the grains have soaked, rinse and drain in a fine-mesh strainer. The liquid that drains off will be thick and cloudy, but this is normal. Be sure to let all the liquid drain out; this will take a few minutes. Set aside.

3. Position the oven rack in the middle of the oven and preheat to 350°F. Line a bread pan with parchment paper so that the parchment paper hangs out over two opposing sides.

4. In a medium bowl mix the psyllium husk with 1½ cups water and set aside for 5 minutes to thicken. This will serve as the main binder for the bread.

5. Add the drained grains, 1½ cups rolled oats, thickened psyllium mix, baking powder, apple cider vinegar, and salt to a food processor and process until the grains are broken up and the mixture is almost smooth. Stop and scrape down the sides of the processor a few times throughout.

(Continued on page 71)

6. Add the remaining ½ cup oats, chia seeds, and hemp seeds to the processor and pulse 10 to 12 times until combined.

7. Transfer the mix to the parchment-paper-lined bread pan. The dough will be thick and sticky. Smooth out the surface of the loaf using the spatula and then use a sharp knife to make shallow diagonal cuts in the surface.

8. Bake the loaf for 40 minutes, then remove the bread from the pan by pulling the parchment paper out of the bread pan. Place the bread directly on the oven rack and continue baking for another 25 to 30 minutes until the bread is browned.

9. Remove the loaf from the oven and place directly on a cooling rack and let cool completely. Once completely cooled, cut into ½- to ¾-inch slices using a sharp knife. If not enjoying this bread within 1 to 2 days, I suggest freezing the slices in single layers separated by parchment paper. When ready to enjoy, toast or double toast the slices right from the freezer.

Blueberry, Banana & Chia Muffins

This muffin needs no intro! It's my favorite everyday muffin that I always have on hand for breakfasts and snacks. Chia seeds add a special texture and bump up the nutritional profile with omega-3 fats, fiber, vitamins, and minerals!

Makes 12 muffins

Ingredients

2 cups gluten-free oat flour

½ cup blanched almond flour

½ cup gluten-free old-fashioned rolled oats

¼ cup chia seeds

2 teaspoons baking powder

½ teaspoon baking soda

1 teaspoon cinnamon

¼ teaspoon ground nutmeg

¾ teaspoon sea salt

2 medium, very ripe bananas (1 cup mashed)

⅓ cup creamy almond butter or preferred nut/seed butter

⅓ cup maple syrup

½ cup unsweetened almond milk or organic soy milk

1 teaspoon pure vanilla extract

1 cup fresh or frozen blueberries

Preparation

1. Position the oven rack in the middle of the oven and preheat to 350°F.

2. In a large bowl, mix together oat flour, almond flour, rolled oats, chia seeds, baking powder, baking soda, cinnamon, nutmeg, and salt.

3. In a medium bowl, mash the bananas until there are no big chunks. Add the nut butter and maple syrup and mix until well combined. Now, add the almond milk and vanilla and mix again.

4. Add the wet ingredients to the dry and mix until no dry spots remain. Then, fold in the blueberries.

5. Scoop out a heaping ⅓ cup of batter into each muffin mold (I use my 3¼-ounce spring-release scoop or disher). Bake in the oven for 23 to 26 minutes until the muffins are almost firm to the touch.

6. Remove the muffins from the oven, place on a cooling rack, and let them cool in the muffin tin for 15 minutes. If using a nonstick muffin tin, use a thin spatula to run along the edge of each muffin and pop them out. If using a silicone muffin pan, let the muffins cool until the pan is no longer hot, then pull the sides of the pan to release the muffins. Place the muffins on the cooling rack and let them cool completely. Keep these muffins in the fridge for 2 to 3 days or in the freezer for up to 3 months.

Mini Buckwheat Bagels

Nonstick silicone donut pans have inspired some fun creations in my kitchen, but these bagels have completely changed how I do brunch! The exact size of your donut pan is important for this recipe. I use 3-inch donut pans with ¼- to ½-inch donut holes. These are popular and widely available. Each pan has six donut molds. If your dimensions are different, fill each donut mold until the batter is flush with the pan's surface. Different donut pans will require different baking times.

Makes 10–12 (3-inch) bagels

Ingredients

¼ cup whole psyllium husk

1¾ cups water

1 cup blanched almond flour

1 cup buckwheat flour

2 tablespoons arrowroot starch

¼ cup chia seeds

¼ cup sesame seeds

1 tablespoon baking powder

1¼ teaspoons sea salt

1 tablespoon apple cider vinegar

> These bagels are best when they're cut in half, toasted, and served with any of the following combinations:
>
> *Our House Hummus + Sliced Cucumber + Pinch Salt*
>
> *Unforgettable French Onion Dip + Sprouts + Red Pepper Flakes*
>
> *Almond Butter + Sliced Banana + Pinch Salt*
>
> *Brilliant Beet Hummus + Sliced Radish + Sesame Seeds*

Preparation

1. Position the oven rack to the middle of the oven and preheat to 350°F.

2. Mix the psyllium husk with 1¾ cups water in a medium-sized bowl. Set aside for 5 minutes to thicken.

3. In a large bowl, mix together the almond flour, buckwheat flour, arrowroot starch, chia seeds, sesame seeds, baking powder, and salt. Break up any clumps of almond flour using a spatula or whisk.

4. Once the psyllium mix has thickened, add it to the large bowl of dry ingredients along with the apple cider vinegar. Using a nonstick spatula, stir the dough together until no dry spots remain. It will be thick.

5. Scoop out about ⅓ cup of the dough and, using damp hands, distribute it evenly into the donut mold so that it's smooth and flush with the pan. Repeat with remaining dough.

6. Place the pans directly on the oven rack and bake for 14 to 16 minutes. They're done when firm to the touch and no wet spots are visible. Once removed from the oven, let them cool in the pans on a cooling rack for 10 minutes. Then, gently pop the bagels out of the pan and let them cool completely on the cooling rack. Keep these in the fridge for up to 3 days or the freezer for up to 3 months.

Banana-Raspberry Breakfast Bake Casserole

This easy oatmeal bake is my go-to brunch recipe! It's creamy and cozy and is just divine with Almond Butter Caramel drizzled over the top! This is also great made ahead of time and reheated for a quick breakfast or even healthy dessert. For this recipe, I don't line my casserole dish with parchment paper.

Makes 6–8 servings

Ingredients

1 teaspoon whole psyllium husk

¼ cup water

3 cups gluten-free old-fashioned rolled oats

¾ cup sliced or chopped almonds

¼ cup hemp seeds

2 teaspoons baking powder

1 teaspoon cinnamon

¼ teaspoon sea salt

2 medium, ripe bananas

¼ cup maple syrup

1 teaspoon pure vanilla extract

2½ –3 cups unsweetened almond milk or organic soy milk

2½ cups fresh or frozen raspberries

Almond Butter Caramel (page 45), optional

Berries and maple syrup for serving

Variations: Try blueberries or blackberries instead of raspberries. For a nut-free version, use pumpkin seeds instead of almonds and skip the Almond Butter Caramel.

Preparation

1. Position the oven rack in the middle of the oven and preheat to 350°F.

2. In a small bowl, mix the psyllium husk with ¼ cup of water and set aside for 5 minutes to thicken.

3. In a large bowl mix the oats, almonds, hemp seeds, baking powder, cinnamon, and salt.

4. In a separate large bowl, mash the bananas until there are no big chunks but some texture remains. Add the thickened psyllium mix, maple syrup, vanilla, and almond milk (2½ cups milk for firmer texture and 3 cups for looser) to the bowl of mashed bananas and mix well. Add this wet mixture to the bowl of dry ingredients and mix until well combined. Fold in the raspberries.

5. Pour the batter into a square 9-inch casserole dish (or similar size). Bake the oatmeal, uncovered, for 45 to 60 minutes or until the top of the oatmeal begins to brown and the middle of the bake is no longer wet. Let the bake cool for 10 minutes before serving, it will firm as it cools. Divide among bowls and serve with Almond Butter Caramel, maple syrup, and/or fresh berries.

SOUPS & STEWS
LIGHT & FILLING, HEALING & WHOLESOME

Hydrating and nourishing. Eat soup often. Here you'll find a combination of pureed, broth-y, and chunky soups that you can enjoy any time of year.

Veggie-forward soups are an easy way to upgrade your diet and consume more nutrients. Like salads, soups allow you to mix any veggies, spices, beans, or grains—they're easy, breezy, and forgiving.

Although soups are easy to make, it's important to choose a quality vegetable broth, make your own, or even use water (with adjusted spices and seasoning). I use my no-salt added Homemade Vegetable Broth (page 81) in all the recipes in this book. If you use premade vegetable broth, be aware of its sodium content and adjust salt accordingly for each recipe.

Homemade Vegetable Broth   81

Golden Garlic & Cauliflower Soup   82

Warming Carrot & Tomato Soup   85

Sweet Potato Rosemary Bisque   86

Cleansing Turnip & Fennel Soup   89

Thai Curry Noodle Soup   90

Soothing Winter Squash & Miso Stew   93

Sunday Tempeh Stew   95

Smoky Chickpea Stew with Cherry Tomatoes & Kale   97

Indian Split Pea Soup   100

Lentil Butternut Squash Stew   103

Homemade Vegetable Broth

Vegetable broth is the foundation for soups, stews, and sauces! Think of broth as the first layer of flavor—it adds depth to any recipe. Making your own allows you to control the ingredients, not to mention save money! I don't add any salt to my broth, preferring to add it as needed when cooking. This recipe is very forgiving. Add or take away any spice or veggie. There's pretty much no way you can mess it up. I keep a few liters frozen in my freezer at all times. If you have the freezer space, it's worth the effort!

Makes 8 cups broth

Ingredients

2 onions, chopped

2 large carrots, chopped

3 celery stalks, chopped

Handful of mushrooms (fresh or dried)

2 tomatoes, chopped

6 garlic cloves, peeled and crushed

1-inch piece fresh ginger, sliced

15 black peppercorns

5–8 sprigs fresh thyme or 1 teaspoon dried thyme

1 small bunch parsley

1 (3-inch) piece kombu

4 bay leaves

12 cups water

Preparation

1. Add all the ingredients to a large pot and bring to a boil. Once boiling, reduce to a simmer, partially cover, and simmer for 1 to 1½ hours.

2. Remove the pot from heat and let it cool. Once cool enough to handle, drain the broth from the veggies in a fine-mesh strainer. I like to use a spatula to press out any extra broth. Transfer the broth to sealed containers and keep in the fridge for up to 5 days or in the freezer for up to 3 months.

Variations: I also add any leftover veggie scraps from asparagus stems to zucchini peels. You can add any fresh or dried herb you like. If you don't have fresh herbs, you can omit and still make a great broth!

Golden Garlic & Cauliflower Soup

A truly healing soup starring anti-inflammatory ginger, turmeric, garlic, and cauliflower. The flavor-enhancing ingredient is roasted garlic, and even though 15 cloves seems like a lot, once roasted, the garlic mellows and imparts incredible flavor. This is a hydrating pureed soup that I make whenever I'm feeling under the weather. For a more filling version, add beans, grains, or greens.

Makes 3–4 servings

Ingredients

1 cup diced yellow onion

½ teaspoon ground turmeric

3 cups bite-sized cauliflower florets (½ medium head cauliflower)

4 cups low-sodium vegetable broth

15 roasted garlic cloves, peeled (see Roasting Garlic how-to below)

2 tablespoons well-stirred tahini

2 teaspoons finely grated ginger

2 tablespoons freshly squeezed lemon juice

Pinch cayenne or to your preference

½ teaspoon sea salt or to taste

Black pepper

Optional Additions
1½ cups chickpeas, 2 cups baby spinach
Optional Garnishes
Fresh herbs, sesame seeds, tahini

Roasting Garlic

Preheat the oven to 400°F. Keep the peel on the garlic cloves and pierce each clove with a paring knife (this keeps the garlic cloves from exploding in the oven). Place the garlic cloves on a sheet pan in the oven and roast for 16 to 20 minutes or until the garlic is browned and fragrant. Remove from the oven and let cool. When cool enough to handle, peel the garlic and use according to recipe.

Preparation

1. In a large pot, sauté the onion with a few tablespoons of water and a pinch of salt for 10 minutes or until the onions are completely translucent and starting to caramelize. Stir often and add water as needed to prevent burning. Add the turmeric and cauliflower and continue to sauté for another couple of minutes.

2. Add the vegetable broth and bring to a boil. Once boiling, reduce to a simmer, cover, and simmer for 12 to 15 minutes until the cauliflower is tender.

3. Turn the heat off and carefully transfer the soup to a high-speed blender (in batches if needed). Add the roasted garlic, tahini, ginger, lemon juice, cayenne, and salt to the blender and blend until completely smooth.

4. Return the soup to the pot. Taste and reseason with salt and pepper if needed. For a heartier version, add chickpeas and spinach to the pot and warm over low heat. Garnish with fresh herbs, sesame seeds, or a drizzle of tahini.

Warming Carrot & Tomato Soup

I loved pureed tomato soup as a kid (unfortunately, it was the canned kind). This version is a massive nutritional upgrade! It's thickened with carrots and rolled oats and has a bright, tangy finish thanks to lemon juice and warming ginger.

Makes 4–6 servings

Ingredients

1 cup diced yellow onion

4 garlic cloves, minced

2 cups roughly chopped carrots (2–3 carrots)

⅓ cup gluten-free old-fashioned rolled oats

1¾ teaspoon ground cumin

¾ teaspoon cinnamon

¼ teaspoon red pepper flakes or to your preference

1 (28 ounce) can diced tomatoes

2 tablespoons tomato paste

4 cups low-sodium vegetable broth

2 teaspoons finely grated ginger

1 tablespoon freshly squeezed lemon juice

½ teaspoon sea salt or to taste

Optional Garnishes

Pumpkin seeds, Hickory Almond Parmesan (page 149), Bacon-ish Bits (page 116)

Nutritional Nugget

Lycopene is a powerful antioxidant found in tomatoes and tomato paste (and other pink/red fruits and vegetables). It's best absorbed when cooked and consumed with some fat, making a drizzle of tahini or a tablespoon of seeds an ideal garnish for this soup!

Procedure

1. In a large pot, sauté the onions with a few tablespoons of water for 5 to 7 minutes or until they're translucent. Add more water as needed.

2. Add the garlic, carrots, and oats and continue to sauté for another 5 minutes, stirring often, and adding water as needed to prevent burning.

3. Add the cumin, cinnamon, and red pepper flakes and sauté for another minute.

4. Now, add the diced tomatoes, tomato paste, and broth, and bring to a boil. Once boiling, reduce to a simmer, and simmer uncovered for 20 to 25 minutes until the carrots are tender. Stir and scrape the bottom of the pot often with a wooden spoon to keep the oats from sticking.

5. Finally, add the grated ginger, lemon juice, and salt and stir. Turn the heat off.

6. Carefully transfer the soup to a high-speed blender (in batches if needed) and blend until completely smooth.

7. Divide among bowls and garnish as you wish! Bacon-ish Bits are an especially delicious addition!

Variations: Add 1½ cups of cooked beans to the soup after blending for a heartier version. Or add a big dollop of Our House Hummus (page 132) or Sour Cream (page 97) to each bowl.

Sweet Potato Rosemary Bisque

This soup is absolutely dreamy! The flavor will make guests think you labored all day over the stove, yet it's incredibly easy to make. There are two secrets to this soup: using fresh rosemary for rich flavor and blending whole almonds into the soup to give it a velvety-smooth finish. I like to serve this as an appetizer or for lunch paired with a salad.

Makes 4–6 servings

Ingredients

1 cup diced yellow onion

4 garlic cloves, minced

3½–4 cups peeled and diced sweet potatoes (about 2 sweet potatoes)

2 packed tablespoons fresh rosemary leaves

½ teaspoon ground sage

3½ cups low-sodium vegetable broth (plus more if needed)

¼ cup almonds, soaked in water for 6–8 hours

1 cup water

2 tablespoons freshly squeezed lemon juice

2–3 teaspoons maple syrup, optional

½ teaspoon sea salt or to taste

Black pepper

Garnish
Fresh rosemary, toasted almonds, cashew cream (see tip below), pepper

---

Tip: Cashew Cream

When I'm really looking to impress, I like to garnish soups with a swirl of tahini or cashew cream. Make cashew cream by adding a 1:1 ratio of cashews to water and a pinch of salt to a high-speed blender and blend until smooth. Add more water to thin if desired.

Preparation

1. In a large pot, sauté the onion with a few tablespoons of water for 5 to 7 minutes until the onion is translucent. Add the garlic, sweet potatoes, rosemary, and sage and continue to sauté for another minute.

2. Now add the vegetable broth, cover, and bring to a boil. Once boiling, reduce to a simmer, and simmer covered for 15 to 20 minutes or until the sweet potatoes are very tender. Remove the soup from the heat and carefully transfer the soup (in batches if needed) to a high-speed blender and blend until completely smooth. Return the soup to the pot. Don't rinse the blender, because you'll use it again.

3. Drain the almonds, discard the soaking liquid, and place the almonds in the blender with 1 cup water (or 1 cup additional vegetable broth). Blend the almonds on high for a minute or until completely smooth.

4. Pour the almond milk into the pot. This is my favorite part! The swirl of orange and creamy white is beautiful. Warm the soup over low heat and add the lemon juice, maple syrup (if using), salt, and pepper to taste. Add more vegetable broth to thin the soup if desired. Garnish and serve!

Cleansing Turnip & Fennel Soup

This nutrient-rich soup is perfect after times of indulgence, when you're looking for something light but still comforting and tasty. Fresh fennel and spices make this soup wonderfully flavorful and satisfying. Keep this all-veggie soup in rotation.

Makes 4 servings

Ingredients

1 large yellow onion, diced

2 carrots, diced

2 celery stalks, diced

1 large fennel bulb, trimmed and diced

5 garlic cloves, minced

1 tablespoon ground fennel seed

2 teaspoons dried oregano

1 teaspoon dried basil

¼ teaspoon red pepper flakes or to your preference

1 medium turnip, peeled and diced (about 4 cups)

1 tablespoon tomato paste

6 cups low-sodium vegetable broth

1 tablespoon freshly squeezed lemon juice

1 cup finely chopped kale or baby spinach

½ teaspoon sea salt or to taste

Black pepper

Fennel

The star ingredient of this soup is fennel—both fresh fennel bulb and fennel seed—with the seeds having a more intense flavor. Fennel is very aromatic and has a distinct, licorice-like taste. Fresh fennel has three parts: bulb, stalks, and fronds. I like to add fennel stalks to soup stocks and use the fronds in salads or as a garnish. If you've never tried fennel, this is a great recipe to start with.

Preparation

1. In a large pot, sauté the onion, carrots, celery, and fennel bulb with about ¼ cup water for 7 to 10 minutes, adding water as needed to prevent burning.

2. Add the garlic, ground fennel seed, oregano, basil, and red pepper flakes. Stir and sauté for another couple of minutes.

3. Now, add the turnip, tomato paste, and broth and bring to a boil. Once boiling, reduce to a simmer and simmer, partially covered, for 40 minutes until the turnip is tender.

4. Add the lemon juice, greens, and salt and turn the heat off. The greens will wilt quickly. Taste and reseason with salt and pepper and serve.

Variations: If turnip is unavailable, use sweet potato or butternut squash. Add white beans or chickpeas for a heartier soup.

Thai Curry Noodle Soup

I love curry soups and Thai dishes, but most are made with curry pastes and coconut milk and I don't use too much of either. This soup is made with quality curry powder, lemongrass, and cashews. It's one of our favorite noodle soups! For this recipe you have to press the tofu and soak cashews ahead of time.

Makes 4–6 servings

Ingredients

1 (12–14 ounce) package extra-firm organic tofu, pressed (see page 17 for how-to), cut into ¾-inch cubes

½ cup cashews, soaked in water for 2–3 hours

1 yellow onion, diced

4 garlic cloves, minced

1 tablespoon finely grated ginger

1 Thai chili, thinly sliced (omit for less spicy)

1 large red bell pepper, deseeded and cut into thin strips

6 ounces shiitake or cremini mushrooms, thinly sliced

2 tablespoons curry powder (mild for less spicy)

2 (4-inch) pieces of lemongrass, halved lengthwise

6 cups low-sodium vegetable broth

3 cups bite-sized broccoli florets

2 nests (3.5 ounces) brown rice vermicelli noodles

2–3 tablespoons tamari

2–3 tablespoons freshly squeezed lime juice

Optional Garnishes

1 bunch cilantro or mint, sliced scallions, siracha, sliced red pepper, enoki mushrooms

Variations: Increase the cashews to 1 cup for a creamier soup or reduce for a lighter version. Omit the cashews for a clear broth or nut-free option.

Preparations

1. While pressing the tofu and soaking the cashews, prepare all the vegetables and set aside.

2. In a large pot, sauté the onion with a few tablespoons of water for 5 to 7 minutes or until the onion is translucent. Add the garlic, ginger, Thai chili, red pepper, mushrooms, and curry powder and continue to sauté for another 3 to 5 minutes, adding water as needed.

3. Add the lemongrass and vegetable broth and bring to a boil. Once boiling, reduce to a simmer and simmer, partially covered, for 10 minutes.

4. Now, add the cubed tofu and broccoli and simmer, partially covered, for another 5 minutes until the broccoli is bright green and tender. Add the vermicelli noodles and stir.

5. Turn the heat off and remove 1 cup of broth from the pot and transfer to a high-speed blender. Drain the cashews, discard the soaking water, and add them to the blender with the broth. Blend until completely smooth. Return the cashew blend to the pot and stir in 2 tablespoons each tamari and lime juice. Remove and discard the lemongrass stalks. Taste and adjust tamari and lime as needed. The noodles should be cooked by now.

6. Divide the soup among bowls (use tongs to get the veggies and noodles and a ladle for the broth). Garnish as you wish!

Soothing Winter Squash & Miso Stew

Miso soups are comforting and good for the gut! This one is a hearty, winter-inspired, and thick soup-stew hybrid. You can use your favorite winter squash and either dried adzuki beans (red mung beans) or navy beans. This recipe requires soaking the rice and dry beans overnight, allowing for faster cooking and better digestion.

Makes 4–6 servings

Ingredients

½ cup dry adzuki beans or dry navy beans

½ cup dry short- or long-grain brown rice

1 large yellow onion, diced

3 celery stalks, diced

3 medium carrots, diced

5 garlic cloves, minced

6 ounces cremini or button mushrooms, sliced

3 cups (1-inch chunks) kabocha, acorn, or butternut squash*

7 cups low-sodium vegetable broth (plus more if needed)

1 tablespoon tamari

2 teaspoons finely grated ginger

1 tablespoon freshly squeezed lemon juice

2 tablespoons white miso

1 packed cup finely chopped kale, Swiss chard, or baby spinach

---

Tip: Miso

Add miso at the end of cooking soups and avoid boiling to preserve the beneficial bacteria that make miso healthy for the gut and digestive system.

Preparation

1. Place the adzuki beans and brown rice in a large bowl and cover with water. Let the beans and rice soak overnight or for at least 8 hours then drain, rinse, and set aside.

2. In a large soup pot, sauté the onion, celery, and carrots with about ¼ cup of water for 7 to 10 minutes, stirring often, until the onion has softened. Add water as needed to prevent burning.

3. Add the garlic and mushrooms and sauté for another few minutes.

4. Add the squash, drained beans and rice, and vegetable broth and bring the soup to a boil. Once boiling, reduce to a simmer, partially cover, and simmer for 1 to 1½ hours, stirring occasionally, until the beans are tender. Mix in the tamari, ginger, and lemon juice. Turn the heat off.

5. Remove ½ cup of the soup and mix with the miso in a small bowl until the miso is dissolved. Return the mixture to the pot and stir to combine. Add the greens and let the soup sit for a few minutes. Add more broth to thin the stew if desired. Taste, reseason, and serve.

---

*If using kabocha or acorn squash, leave the peel on, but butternut squash should be peeled.

Sunday Tempeh Stew

Sundays are a slow day in my book and this is my favorite stew to make for a laid-back, nourishing meal to share with family on a Sunday evening. You start by sautéing the tempeh in a marinade and then move onto the stew. It's delicious and comes together easily. It's even better left over!

Makes 4–6 servings

Ingredients

Tempeh

2 tablespoons tamari

2 tablespoons balsamic vinegar

1 (8 ounce) package tempeh, cut into ¾-inch cubes

Stew

2 medium yellow onions, diced

2 large celery stalks, thinly sliced

2 large carrots, sliced into ¼-inch rounds

¼ cup brown rice flour

5 garlic cloves, minced

2 teaspoons dried rosemary

1¾ teaspoons dried thyme

¼ teaspoon red pepper flakes or to your preference

⅛ teaspoon ground allspice

¼ cup tomato paste

5 red potatoes, peel on, chopped into 1-inch cubes

6 cups low-sodium vegetable broth

1 tablespoon tamari

2 teaspoons balsamic vinegar

Sea salt and black pepper to taste

Preparation

1. First, marinate the tempeh. Mix 2 tablespoons each of tamari and balsamic vinegar in a container with a lid and add the cubed tempeh. Cover the container and flip it a couple of times to coat all the tempeh. Let the tempeh marinate for 20 minutes, flipping the container a few times throughout. While the tempeh is marinating, chop the veggies.

2. After 20 minutes, add the tempeh and the marinade to a large soup pot and cook on low to medium heat, stirring, for 3 to 5 minutes until the tempeh begins to brown and the marinade has evaporated. Add water as needed to prevent sticking. Transfer the cooked tempeh to a plate and set aside.

3. Without rinsing the pot, add the onions, celery, and carrots to the pot with about ¼ cup water. Sauté on medium heat for 10 minutes or until the onions are translucent. Stir often and add water as needed to prevent burning. Sprinkle in the brown rice flour and stir to coat all the veggies.

4. Now, add the garlic, dried spices, and tomato paste and sauté for another minute, stirring to mix in the tomato paste and scraping the bottom of the pan with your spoon to prevent the flour from sticking.

(Continued on next page)

5. Add the potatoes and vegetable broth. Bring to a boil. Once boiling, reduce to a simmer, partially cover, and simmer for 35 minutes or until the potatoes and carrots are tender.

6. Remove from heat, add the remaining tablespoon of tamari, 2 teaspoons of balsamic vinegar, and the cooked tempeh. Stir, taste, and reseason with tamari (or salt), and black pepper. Let the stew rest for 5 minutes before serving.

Variations: Other veggies that work well in this stew include parsnips, turnips, and mushrooms.

Smoky Chickpea Stew with Cherry Tomatoes & Kale

A simple, smoky stew that makes wonderful use of cherry tomatoes, especially when they're in season. I like to add a dollop of Sour Cream or diced avocado to make it extra special!

Makes 3–4 servings

Ingredients

2 medium yellow onions, diced

6 garlic cloves, minced

1 tablespoon ground cumin

1½ teaspoons smoked paprika

2 cups cherry tomatoes, halved

3 tablespoons tomato paste

1 medium red potato, peel on, chopped into 1-inch cubes

1½ cups cooked or canned chickpeas, drained and rinsed

3 cups low-sodium vegetable broth (more if needed)

1 tablespoon nutritional yeast

2 cups roughly chopped kale

½ teaspoon sea salt or to taste

Sour Cream (see recipe below) or chopped avocado, optional

Sour Cream

1 cup cashews, soaked in water for 2–3 hours

1 tablespoon apple cider vinegar

¾ teaspoon Dijon mustard

¼ teaspoon sea salt

½ cup water

Preparation

1. In a large pot, sauté the onions with a few tablespoons of water for 5 to 7 minutes until the onions become translucent. Add more water as needed to prevent burning.

2. Add the garlic, cumin, smoked paprika, cherry tomatoes, and tomato paste and continue to sauté, stirring, for another 2 minutes.

3. Next, add the potato, chickpeas, and broth and bring to a boil. Once boiling, reduce to a simmer and simmer partially covered for 25 to 30 minutes, stirring occasionally and breaking up the tomatoes with the back of a wooden spoon.

4. While the stew is cooking, make the Sour Cream (if using). Drain the cashews, discard the soaking liquid, and add the drained cashews, apple cider vinegar, Dijon mustard, salt, and water to a high-speed blender. Blend on high until completely smooth. Transfer to a glass container.

5. Finish the stew by adding the nutritional yeast, kale, and salt. Stir and turn the heat off. Let the kale wilt for a few minutes. Taste and reseason. Divide among bowls and top with a dollop of Sour Cream or chopped avocado if desired.

(Continued on page 99)

Variations: Use butternut squash, pumpkin or sweet potato instead of regular potato.

Recipe Recycle: Leftover soup will get even thicker and is delicious warmed and served over brown rice.

Tip: Saving Tomato Paste

How often have you opened a can of tomato paste, used a few tablespoons, and wondered what to do with the rest? Here's a life hack: measure individual 1-tablespoon servings of the remaining tomato paste, place them on parchment paper or a silicone baking mat, and lay on a flat surface in the freezer. Once frozen, transfer the tablespoon servings to a freezer safe container and add to future recipes as needed. Money-saving culinary wisdom!

Indian Split Pea Soup

This soup has been in my repertoire for almost ten years! It's one of those cold-night, wool socks, warm-me-up kind of soups. I suggest soaking the split peas overnight to shorten cooking time. When the soup is ready, the sweet potatoes and split peas will have melted into a creamy consistency. As always, add greens for an extra nutritional boost and pop of color.

Makes 6 servings

Ingredients

2 medium yellow onions, diced

2 medium carrots, diced

2 celery stalks, diced

4 garlic cloves, minced

3 medium sweet potatoes, peel on, diced
    (about 6 cups)

1 tablespoon ground cumin

1 tablespoon ground coriander

1½ teaspoons garam masala

½ teaspoon ground turmeric

Pinch red pepper flakes (more if desired)

1¼ cups yellow split peas, soaked overnight

8 cups low-sodium vegetable broth (plus more if
    needed)

1 tablespoon finely grated ginger

2 tablespoons freshly squeezed lemon juice

2 cups packed baby spinach or chopped kale or
    Swiss chard

¾ teaspoon sea salt or to taste

Black pepper

Grinding Spices

You can grind your own whole spices and seeds using an inexpensive coffee grinder. This way your ground spices and seeds are as fresh as possible which translates to tastier (and healthier) meals.

Preparation

1. In a large pot, sauté the onions, carrots, and celery with about ¼ cup water for 7 to 10 minutes or until the onions become translucent. Add more water as needed to prevent burning.

2. Add the garlic, sweet potatoes, and spices and sauté for another few minutes.

3. Drain the split peas, discard the soaking water, and add the drained split peas to the pot along with the vegetable broth. Cover and bring to a boil. Once boiling, reduce to a simmer and simmer, covered, on low to medium heat for 1 to 1½ hours, stirring occasionally until the sweet potato has melted into soup and the split peas are tender or dissolved.

4. Turn the heat off, add the grated ginger, lemon juice, greens, and salt. Stir, taste, and reseason with salt and pepper. You can thin the soup with extra broth if desired.

Lentil Butternut Squash Stew

This stew is creamy, chunky, and loaded with antioxidants. Be sure to chop and prep all the veggies before starting this recipe. The butternut squash can be a little labor intensive and might take longer than expected if you're not familiar with this delightful winter squash.

Makes 4–6 servings

Ingredients

1 large yellow onion, diced

2 celery stalks, thinly sliced

3 medium carrots, diced

5 cloves garlic, minced

1 tablespoon + 2 teaspoons ground cumin

2 teaspoons ground coriander

1 teaspoon dried oregano

¼ teaspoon red pepper flakes or to your preference

1 medium butternut squash, peeled and chopped into 1-inch cubes (about 6 cups)

1 cup dry green or brown lentils, picked over and rinsed

6 cups low-sodium vegetable broth

3 tablespoons well-stirred creamy almond butter

2 teaspoons tamari

2 teaspoons finely grated ginger

2 tablespoons freshly squeezed lemon juice

3 cups baby spinach

½ teaspoon sea salt or more to taste

Preparation

1. In a large pot, sauté the onion, celery, and carrots with about ¼ cup water for 7 to 10 minutes until the onions are translucent. Add water as needed to prevent burning.

2. Add the garlic and all spices and continue to sauté for another 2 minutes.

3. Now, add the squash, lentils, and vegetable broth and bring to a boil. Once boiling, reduce to a simmer and simmer, partially covered, for 30 minutes or until the squash is very tender and lentils are cooked.

4. Remove ½ cup of the broth from the soup and whisk together with the almond butter in a small bowl until a loose paste is formed. Stir the paste into the soup and then add the tamari, ginger, lemon juice, spinach, and salt. Stir, taste, and reseason if necessary.

Variations: For a nut-free version, use tahini or sunflower seed butter instead of almond butter.

Nutritional Nugget

Lentils are one of my favorite plant-based sources of iron. In a single cup of cooked lentils there's over 6 mg of iron, not to mention almost 18 grams of protein! Lentils are cheap, easy to cook, and an essential pantry legume!

SENSATIONAL SALADS
CHOPPED, ROASTED & TOSSED

Traditionally viewed as a mix of raw veggies, "I'll just have the salad" sometimes means settling for something boring, scarce, or wimpy. Not with these salads! Nutrient-dense, filling, and bursting with intense flavors, these salads are chopped, roasted, pickled, crunchy, creamy, tangy, and spicy.

I regularly dive into a version of the Loaded Lunch Salad (page 107) on weekdays and I take every opportunity to serve my Tahini Caesar (page 113) to anyone who thinks vegan salads are dull.

The key to an amazing salad is a great dressing or sauce —a transformative tool! Feel free to mix and match and double batch.

You don't always need a recipe either! A salad is an opportunity to get creative and be resourceful. Let your taste buds and what's in your fridge be your guide. For inspiration, special occasions, and new flavor combinations, try these—my beloved, sensational salads.

Loaded Lunch Salad with Creamy Hemp-Balsamic Dressing　　107

Warm Harvest Salad with Walnut Dressing　　108

The Summer Salad　　111

Tahini Caesar with Quick Smoked Chickpeas & Bacon-ish Bits　　113

Bacon-ish Bits　　116

Greek Salad with Sun-Dried-Tomato Tofu Feta　　119

Strawberry Spinach Salad with White-Balsamic Dressing　　123

Pad Thai Protein Salad　　125

Quick Pickled Cucumber Side Salad with Chickpeas　　127

Loaded Lunch Salad with Creamy Hemp-Balsamic Dressing

I have a salad almost every day for lunch, and this is my go-to combination. An important tip for making enjoyable salads is to chop the veggies small—big chunks of raw veggies can be off-putting or difficult to digest. The tangy and nutrient-dense Creamy Hemp-Balsamic Dressing is a perfect house salad dressing! Adjust the quinoa and beans according to your hunger.

Makes 1–2 salads (with leftover dressing)

Ingredients

Hemp-Balsamic Dressing
2 pitted Medjool dates, soaked in hot water for 15–30 minutes
3 tablespoons hemp seeds
3 tablespoons balsamic vinegar
3 tablespoons freshly squeezed orange juice
2 tablespoons smooth Dijon mustard (not grainy)
2 teaspoons tamari

Salad
3 cups leafy greens (baby lettuce, arugula, or spinach)
⅓ cup shredded red cabbage
1 small carrot, peeled into strips
¼ cup thinly sliced cucumber
¼ cup quartered cherry tomatoes
½ cup finely chopped broccoli or cauliflower
¼–½ cup cooked quinoa
¼–½ cup cooked chickpeas, lentils, or black beans or a big scoop of hummus
Pinch dulse flakes, optional
1–2 tablespoons nuts, seeds, or Bacon-ish Bits (page 116), optional

Preparation

1. First make the dressing. Drain the dates, reserving the soaking liquid, and add the drained dates, hemp seeds, balsamic vinegar, orange juice, Dijon, and tamari to the blender. Add 1 tablespoon of soaking liquid and blend on high until smooth. Add more soaking liquid (or water) as needed to reach a pourable consistency. This dressing is ideally made in a smaller blender. If using a large blender, stop and scrape down the sides a couple of times throughout blending or double the batch.

2. To assemble, add all the salad ingredients to a large bowl or arrange them in sections and drizzle with dressing. Store leftover dressing in the fridge for up to 3 days.

Warm Harvest Salad with Walnut Dressing

A wholesome salad designed for the colder months. This is a warm, grain-based salad that highlights one of my favorite health-supportive, cruciferous veggies, brussels sprouts! Soaking the walnuts makes for a creamier consistency and better digestion.

Makes 4 servings

Ingredients

Salad

1 cup dry brown rice

4 heaping cups brussels sprouts, quartered or halved

1 large sweet potato, peel on, chopped the same size as brussels sprouts

1 stalk celery, thinly sliced

½ Granny Smith apple, peel on or off, finely diced

⅓ cup dried cranberries

Walnut Dressing

½ cup walnuts, soaked in water for 2–3 hours

2 tablespoons red wine vinegar

1 tablespoon Dijon mustard

1½ teaspoons maple syrup, optional

1 small garlic clove, minced

¾ teaspoon dried rosemary

¾ teaspoon dehydrated minced onion

¼ teaspoon sea salt

½ cup water

Optional Garnish

Chopped walnuts

Tip: Dried Herbs

When using dried leafy herbs like rosemary, oregano, or thyme, rub them between your hands before adding to the recipe. This "wakes" them up and releases more flavor!

Preparation

1. First, cook the rice according to package directions. Once cooked, fluff with a fork, cover, and set aside. Meanwhile, preheat the oven to 425°F. Line a baking sheet with parchment paper.

2. Spread the brussels sprouts and sweet potato onto the pan in a single layer and bake in the oven for 30 to 35 minutes, flipping halfway through. The veggies are done when the sweet potato is tender and the brussels sprouts are browned and charred on the edges.

3. While waiting for the veggies and rice, make the dressing. Drain the walnuts, discard the soaking water, and add the walnuts to a high-speed blender along with all other dressing ingredients. Blend on high until completely smooth.

4. To assemble the salad, add the warm rice, roasted veggies, celery, apple, and cranberries to a large salad bowl. Add half the dressing and toss. Divide among bowls, drizzle with extra dressing, and garnish with walnuts.

The Summer Salad

This fresh and vibrant salad has everything, and you can bring it anywhere—it's multipurpose. It's ideal for potlucks, picnics, and summer BBQs, and it serves as an easy side dish or nutrient-packed lunch! A simple dressing made of lime juice and spices gives this salad depth of flavor while still being light. If making the salad ahead of time, wait to add the avocado and spinach until just before serving.

Makes 4–6 servings

Ingredients

⅓ cup freshly squeezed lime juice

¾ teaspoon chili powder

½ teaspoon smoked paprika

⅛ teaspoon cayenne pepper, optional

½ teaspoon sea salt

2 cups cooked and cooled quinoa or brown rice

1½ cups cooked or canned black beans or chickpeas (or a combination), drained and rinsed

½ cup finely diced red onion

½ cup finely diced red bell pepper

½ cup finely diced yellow bell pepper

1 cup cherry tomatoes, halved

1 heaping cup diced fresh mango (or frozen, thawed and drained)

1 avocado, peeled, pitted, and diced

2 cups baby spinach

Cilantro, optional

Preparation

1. In a small bowl, mix together the lime juice, chili powder, smoked paprika, cayenne, and salt. Set aside.

2. In a large bowl add the quinoa/rice, beans, onion, red and yellow peppers, tomatoes, and mango. Pour in the lime juice/spices and mix to combine. Now, fold in the avocado and baby spinach and gently toss. Taste and reseason with salt and garnish with cilantro if desired.

Tahini Caesar with Quick Smoked Chickpeas & Bacon-ish Bits

Kale Caesar salads are popular for a good reason—they're incredible! Whoever came up with this pairing, one million thank-yous! I like to make mine with a mix of curly kale and crunchy romaine. Tossed with a creamy tahini dressing and then garnished with smoky chickpeas and bacon-ish bits, this salad breaks the salad mold and is undeniably delicious. After the kale and romaine is washed, pat dry to allow the dressing to better coat the leaves.

Makes 4 servings

Ingredients

Tahini Caesar Dressing
⅓ cup well-stirred tahini
3 tablespoons freshly squeezed lemon juice
1 teaspoon apple cider vinegar
2 small garlic cloves
2 tablespoons capers, drained
1½ teaspoons Dijon mustard
1 teaspoon nutritional yeast
1 teaspoon maple syrup, optional
Pinch sea salt
Pinch black pepper
¼ cup water

Quick Smoked Chickpeas
1½ cups cooked or canned chickpeas, drained and
    rinsed
2 teaspoons dehydrated minced onion

¾ teaspoon smoked paprika
Pinch red pepper flakes or to your preference
½ teaspoon coconut sugar, optional
2 teaspoons tamari
1 teaspoon balsamic vinegar
2 tablespoons water

Salad
1 large bunch curly kale, stems removed, chopped
    (6 packed cups)
Lemon slice
 1 large head romaine lettuce (hearts and leaves),
    chopped (5 packed cups)
½ cup Bacon-ish Bits (page 116) or Cashew
    Turmeric Parmesan (page 149)

(Continued on next page)

Preparation

1. First, make the Tahini Caesar Dressing. Add all dressing ingredients to a blender and blend until smooth. Add more water as needed, 1 tablespoon at a time, to reach a smooth pourable consistency. Taste and reseason with salt and pepper. Set aside.

2. Next, make the Quick Smoked Chickpeas. Add the chickpeas and all other ingredients to a medium-sized pot and sauté over medium heat for 3 to 5 minutes, stirring often until the spices are fragrant and all the water has evaporated. Cover and set aside.

3. Then, prepare the salad. Add the chopped kale to a large bowl and add a squeeze of lemon juice. Massage the kale with your hands for about a minute until the leaves soften, shrink in size, and turn bright green. This softens the fibers and improves the flavor. Now, add the chopped romaine to the bowl, mix, and drizzle half the dressing over the greens. Toss until all the greens are coated (you can use your hands to do this too!). Add as much dressing as is desired, saving a little for garnish.

4. Time to assemble! Add the warm smoked chickpeas to the salad and a final drizzle of dressing. Garnish with Bacon-ish Bits or Cashew Turmeric Parmesan. Toss again and serve.

Variations: Skip the chickpeas and add Balsamic Tempeh (page 175) or Fresh Falafel (page 171) instead. Or for a quicker version, omit the chickpeas altogether.

Recipe Recycle: The tahini sauce makes an amazing sauce for roasted veggies or cooked grains and is delicious on Blackout Burgers (page 185).

Bacon-ish Bits

Smoky, savory, a little sweet, and a lot of crunch! I use this almond and sunflower seed mix as a tasty topping for salads, pastas, and soups. They're magic! Go ahead, make a triple batch.

Makes 1 cup

Ingredients

1 teaspoon smoked paprika

½ teaspoon onion powder

½ teaspoon garlic powder

1 teaspoon nutritional yeast

1 tablespoon + 1 teaspoon tamari

1 teaspoon maple syrup, optional

½ cup sliced almonds

½ cup sunflower seeds

Preparation

1. Preheat the oven to 300°F and line a baking sheet with parchment paper.

2. In a medium-sized bowl, mix the spices, nutritional yeast, tamari, and maple syrup (if using) into a paste.

3. Now, add the almonds and sunflower seeds and mix well using a nonstick spatula until all the nuts and seeds are coated.

4. Transfer the almonds and sunflower seeds to the baking sheet in a single layer and bake for 18 to 20 minutes, mixing and redistributing into a single layer halfway through. They're done when slightly browned and dry to the touch. Remove from the oven, mix around to break up any clumps, and let cool completely. They'll harden as they cool. Keep these Bacon-ish Bits in a sealed jar in a dry, cool place for up to a month.

Variations: For a nut-free version use pumpkin seeds or another ½ cup of sunflower seeds instead of almonds.

Greek Salad with Sun-Dried-Tomato Tofu Feta

This is an impressive salad layered with incredible Mediterranean flavors. I love Greek salads but don't order them in restaurants very often because they're usually dripping in oil and layered with cheese. So, I prefer to make my own version! Be sure to use extra-firm tofu and dry-packed sun-dried tomatoes, not the variety bottled in oil. The sunflower seeds are ideally soaked for the dressing.

Makes 4 servings

Ingredients

Sun-Dried-Tomato Tofu Feta

1 (12–14 ounce) package extra-firm organic tofu, pressed (see page 17 for how-to)

⅓ cup sun-dried tomatoes, soaked in water for 10 minutes*

2 tablespoons freshly squeezed lemon juice

1 tablespoon red wine vinegar

3 tablespoons nutritional yeast

½ teaspoon dried oregano

½ teaspoon garlic powder

Pinch red pepper flakes

½ teaspoon sea salt

Herbed Sunflower Dressing

¼ cup sunflower seeds, soaked in water for 2–3 hours

2 tablespoons apple cider vinegar

2 tablespoons freshly squeezed lemon juice

1 tablespoon tamari

1 teaspoon onion powder

½ teaspoon dried oregano

½ teaspoon dried basil

1 teaspoon garlic powder

Pinch red pepper flakes

¼ cup + 2 tablespoons water

Salad

2 large heads leafy green or romaine lettuce, chopped

10 Campari tomatoes, sliced or quartered

½ English cucumber, thinly sliced

¾ cup pitted black olives (kalamata are ideal), sliced

½ cup thinly sliced red onion

(Continued on next page)

---

*When soaking the sun-dried tomatoes, use room-temperature water and just enough water to cover them. Hot water or too much water will leach out more of their flavor. You can also use the sun-dried-tomato soaking liquid in the dressing, instead of water, for more flavor!

Preparation

1. First, make the tofu feta. Unwrap the pressed tofu and dice it into ¾-inch cubes. Set aside.

   Drain the sun-dried tomatoes (reserve liquid if using for the dressing) and finely dice.

   In a medium-sized bowl, mix the lemon juice, red wine vinegar, nutritional yeast, oregano, garlic powder, red pepper flakes, and salt and whisk together. Add in the diced sun-dried tomatoes and cubed tofu and toss until all the tofu is coated. Place the tofu feta in the fridge while you make the dressing and salad.

2. Next, make the dressing. Drain the sunflower seeds, discard the soaking liquid, and add the drained sunflower seeds and all other dressing ingredients to a high-speed blender and blend until smooth. Stop and scrape down the sides of the blender one to two times to incorporate all ingredients. Add more water, 1 tablespoon at a time, and blend again if needed to achieve a smooth, pourable consistency.

3. Finally, assemble the salad. Add the lettuce, tomatoes, cucumber, olives, and red onion to a large bowl. Add the tofu feta and drizzle with half the dressing. Toss the salad, divide among bowls, and drizzle with remaining dressing.

Recipe Tips

- For extra-flavorful feta, make the tofu feta one day ahead of time and let it marinate in the fridge overnight.

- If you want a firmer feta, you can steam the diced tofu for 5 minutes and let it cool before adding to the marinade.

- I like to make this dressing in a smaller blender. If using a large blender, double the dressing and save more for later as a dressing for the Loaded Lunch Salad (page 107) or any combination of veggies and grains.

Strawberry Spinach Salad with White-Balsamic Dressing

This is my rendition of a classic salad that I like to serve when strawberries are in season. If I'm eating this as a main meal, I'll add a handful of chickpeas to round out the nutritional profile. For a nut-free version, use toasted sunflower seeds instead of almonds. Be sure to slice the onions razor thin!

Makes 2 main salads or 4 side salads

Ingredients

Salad
⅓ cup sliced almonds
6 cups loosely packed baby spinach
½ cup thinly sliced red onion
2 cups strawberries, thinly sliced

White-Balsamic Dressing
1 tablespoon well-stirred tahini
1 tablespoon + 1 teaspoon Dijon mustard
¾ teaspoon dehydrated minced onion
¼ teaspoon garlic powder
3 tablespoons white balsamic vinegar
1 teaspoon maple syrup, optional
Pinch sea salt
Pinch black pepper

Preparation

1. Place the almonds in a nonstick pan and toast over medium heat, stirring often, for 2 to 4 minutes until the almonds are golden in color and fragrant. Transfer immediately to a plate to cool.

2. While the almonds cool, make the salad dressing by whisking all the dressing ingredients in a small bowl until smooth. Add water, 1 teaspoon at a time, if needed to thin the dressing.

3. Layer the spinach, red onion, strawberries, and toasted almonds in a salad bowl. Drizzle with dressing, toss, and serve.

Pad Thai Protein Salad

Even though it's an inaccurate, outdated debate, there are still some who argue that protein is lacking in a plant-based diet. This creamy, nutrient-dense, eat-the-rainbow inspired salad is proof that whole foods have plenty of protein! If divided into four servings, there's almost 20 grams of protein per serving! This salad is intended to be served at room temperature, but you can serve it warm if preferred. Leftovers make for a wonderful lunch the following day!

Makes 4–6 servings

Ingredients

1 cup frozen organic shelled edamame
1 medium sweet potato, peel on, chopped into
     ½-inch cubes
1 cup bite-sized broccoli florets
1½ cups cooked or canned chickpeas, drained and
     rinsed
1 cup cooked and cooled quinoa
1 medium red bell pepper, diced
½ cup finely shredded red cabbage
½ cup grated or julienned carrot
½ cup diced cucumber
3 scallions, thinly sliced
¼ cup sliced almonds or hemp seeds
1 small bunch cilantro, optional
Lime wedges, for serving

Pad Thai Sauce
¼ cup well-stirred almond butter
1½ teaspoon finely grated ginger
2 tablespoons tamari
1 tablespoon rice wine vinegar
2 tablespoons lime juice
2 teaspoons maple syrup, optional
1 teaspoon vinegar-based hot sauce (more if you
     like it spicy)
1 tablespoon water

Preparation

1. Steam the edamame and sweet potato in a steamer basket for 6 to 8 minutes or until the sweet potato is just about tender. Add the broccoli to the steamer basket and steam for an additional 2 minutes until the broccoli is bright green. Remove the steamer basket from the pot and let the veggies and edamame cool for 10 to 15 minutes.

2. Meanwhile, make the pad thai sauce by adding all ingredients to a small bowl and whisking together using a fork or small whisk until the mixture is smooth. Add more water, 1 teaspoon at time, to thin the sauce as needed. Set aside.

3. Place the cooled edamame, sweet potato, and broccoli in a large salad bowl along with the remaining salad ingredients and mix together. Add the pad thai sauce and toss until well combined. Garnish with additional cilantro, almonds/hemp seeds, or scallions if desired and serve with extra lime wedges.

Recipe Recycle: Pad thai sauce is equally delicious tossed with cooked rice noodles and the same veggies in this recipe.

Quick Pickled Cucumber Side Salad with Chickpeas

This unique side salad packs a sour crunch that complements any rich or hearty main dish. English cucumbers (also known as seedless cucumbers) are ideal for this recipe as they're long and thin (great for making ribbons) and contain less water than other varieties.

Makes 2–3 servings

Ingredients

¼ cup rice wine vinegar

1 garlic clove, minced

½ teaspoon dried dill

1 teaspoon coconut sugar

¼ teaspoon sea salt

1 (12-inch) English cucumber

¼ cup finely diced red onion

1 cup cooked or canned chickpeas, drained and rinsed

Optional Garnishes
Microgreens, fresh dill, sliced almonds

Preparation

1. In a medium-sized bowl, mix together the rice vinegar, garlic, dill, sugar, and salt.

2. Peel the cucumber into thin ribbons using a vegetable peeler or a mandoline. This should yield about 2 heaping cups of cucumber ribbons. Add the cucumber, red onion, and chickpeas to the vinegar mix and toss to coat the cucumber evenly.

3. Set aside for 15 to 20 minutes, tossing again once or twice while pickling. Garnish with microgreens, fresh dill, and/or sliced almonds.

DIPS & SPREADS

DIP, DOLLOP & SMEAR

I simply could not live without dips and spreads made from whole foods! Sometimes I start a meal with a dollop of hummus and build from there.

   Make these recipes for snacks or to share with friends and adjust the flavors to your liking.

   When making bean dips and spreads remember that the temperature of the beans will also affect the consistency. Hot beans will create a seemingly smooth consistency but will firm up once cooled. I like to start my dips and spreads with room-temperature beans and add liquid (water or aquafaba) gradually until a creamy consistency is reached.

Creamy Hummus without Oil?

There are two tips to making creamy hummus without adding oil. First, process the hummus for a long time. I like my hummus smooth and process it continuously for 3 to 4 minutes! Second, use aquafaba (the bean cooking or canned liquid) as the liquid portion in the hummus. You can also use water, but aquafaba adds extra oomph and fluff!

Avocado Tartare   131

Our House Hummus   132

Spring Edamame Green-Pea Hummus   135

Tangy Roasted Red Pepper & Black Bean Spread   136

Spiced Creamy Carrot Hummus   139

Unforgettable French Onion Dip   140

Brilliant Beet Hummus   143

Herbed Cheeze Ball   144

Avocado Tartare

Impressive, delicious, and easy! Creamy avocado, sweet mango, and crunchy cucumber make this tartare actually irresistible. Finely chopping the veggies is key to the tartar sticking together. I like to serve this as an appetizer or snack with whole grain crackers or use it like salsa. It's delicious on Tuesday Tempeh Tacos (page 151).

Makes 3–4 servings

Ingredients

¾ cup peeled and finely diced English cucumber

¼ cup finely diced red onion

¼ cup finely diced fresh mango (or frozen, thawed and drained)

1 small garlic clove, minced

1 teaspoon freshly squeezed lime juice

¼ teaspoon dried dill

Big pinch of sea salt

1 large avocado, pit removed, peeled, chopped into ½-inch cubes

---

Tip

It's best to make this tartare right before serving. If left sitting for too long, it will get watery or, if plated with a mold, lose its shape.

Preparation

1. Place the cucumber, red onion, mango, garlic, lime juice, dill, and salt in a medium-sized bowl. Add the cubed avocado and gently mix so that the cubes maintain their shape. You can serve the tartare in a bowl or you can dress it up by shaping the tartare in a ring mold or packing the tartare into a measuring cup and flipping onto a plate for a nice presentation.

Variations: Try using strawberries instead of mango or 1 tablespoon chopped cilantro instead of dill.

Our House Hummus

This hummus is always in our fridge. Capers are the secret ingredient that make it special with a unique savory finish! I like to smear it on toasted Amazing Multigrain Bread (page 69) or with crudités (fancy word for raw veggies), and Mary's Gone Crackers whole-grain crackers.

Makes 4 cups

Ingredients

3 cups cooked or canned chickpeas, drained and rinsed

3 garlic cloves

¼ cup well-stirred tahini

Scant ¼ cup freshly squeezed lemon juice

2 tablespoons capers, drained

¼ teaspoon sea salt or to taste

¼–½ cup water or aquafaba

What Are Capers?

Capers are small pickled flower buds. They're found next to the pickles and olives and are packed in brine. They give a nice twist to savory recipes.

Preparation

1. Add the chickpeas, garlic, tahini, lemon juice, capers, and salt to a food processor and process continuously. Pour ¼ cup water or aquafaba through the feeding tube while the processor is running. Stop and scrape down the sides to incorporate all ingredients and process again. Add more liquid as needed, 1 tablespoon at a time, to achieve your preferred hummus consistency. I like mine smooth and creamy. Keep this hummus in the fridge for 3 to 5 days.

Variation: Feel free to reduce the tahini for a lighter version. If you're not in love with capers, omit and add ½ teaspoon ground cumin and reseason to taste for a more traditional hummus.

Spring Edamame Green-Pea Hummus

Green, fresh, and creamy. This protein-rich spread is delicious paired with avocado for a spring-inspired avocado toast. Make this spread on repeat!

Makes 4 cups

Ingredients

1½ cups frozen organic shelled edamame

1½ cups frozen green peas

2 garlic cloves

3 tablespoons well-stirred almond butter

3–4 tablespoons freshly squeezed lemon juice

¼ teaspoon red pepper flakes (more if you like it spicy)

½ teaspoon sea salt or to taste

¼–½ cup water

Preparation

1. Add the edamame to a medium pot and cover with 2 to 3 inches of water. Bring the water to a boil. Once boiling, reduce to a rapid simmer for 3 minutes, then add the green peas and continue to simmer for another minute.

2. Drain the edamame and peas and set aside to cool.

3. Once cooled, add the edamame and peas to a food processor along with the garlic, almond butter, lemon juice, red pepper flakes, and salt and process continuously. Pour ¼ cup water through the feeding tube while the processor is running. Scrape down the sides to incorporate all ingredients and process continuously, adding more water as needed to reach a smooth, creamy texture. Taste, reseason, and serve. This will keep in the fridge for 3 to 5 days.

Variations: Use chickpeas instead of edamame or, for a nut-free version, tahini instead of almond butter.

Tangy Roasted Red Pepper
& Black Bean Spread

Red peppers are transformed when they're roasted! They give this black bean hummus a smoky and smooth taste. I like to mix this into warm grains or serve with whole-grain crackers and veggies as a snack or appetizer.

Makes 2 cups

Ingredients

1½ cooked or canned black beans, drained and rinsed

½ packed cup roasted red peppers*

2 tablespoons freshly squeezed lime juice

1½ teaspoons dehydrated minced onion

¾ teaspoon garlic powder

½ teaspoon ground cumin

¼ teaspoon chili powder

¼ teaspoon sea salt or to taste

1–2 chilis in adobo sauce, optional

1–3 tablespoons water or aquafaba

Preparation

1. Add the black beans, roasted red peppers, lime juice, minced onion, garlic powder, cumin, chili powder, salt, red pepper flakes, and chilis in adobo (if using) to a blender or food processor and blend/process until well combined. Add water, 1 tablespoon at a time, to reach your desired consistency. Scrape down the sides to incorporate all ingredients and process again. This will keep in the fridge for 3 to 5 days.

---

*Use roasted red peppers packed in water or roast your own. See page 193 for how-to.

Spiced Creamy Carrot Hummus

This hummus is unique thanks to steamed carrot, spices, and miso! It's a nice change from your regular bean spread. I like it with a little heat, but you can reduce or omit the red pepper flakes (it's still delicious!).

Makes 2½ cups

Ingredients

1 medium carrot, roughly chopped (1 heaping cup)

1½ cups cooked or canned navy beans or chickpeas, drained and rinsed

2 tablespoons well-stirred tahini

2 tablespoons freshly squeezed lemon juice

2 teaspoons white miso

2 garlic cloves

½ teaspoon ground coriander

¼– ½ teaspoon red pepper flakes or to your preference

¼ teaspoon ground cumin

¼ teaspoon sea salt or to taste

2–6 tablespoons water or aquafaba

Preparation

1. Add the chopped carrot to a steamer basket and steam until tender, about 10 to 15 minutes. Let the carrot cool for a few minutes.

2. Add the carrot, beans, tahini, lemon juice, miso, garlic, coriander, red pepper flakes, cumin, and salt to a food processor and process continuously. While processing, add water or aquafaba, gradually, until a creamy consistency is reached. Scrape down the sides to incorporate all ingredients and process again. I like this one really creamy and process for a few minutes. Serve with whole-grain crackers, veggies, or smear on toasted Amazing Multigrain Bread (page 69). This will keep in the fridge for 3 to 5 days.

Unforgettable French Onion Dip

I made this recipe for a cooking class series I taught that was all about the versatility of beans. In every class, this dip/spread was the showstopper! I knew it had to be in a cookbook one day. No one will know this isn't made with cream or cheese! This spread is best made in a high-speed blender.

Makes 3 cups

Ingredients

1 cup cashews, soaked in water for 2–3 hours

1 cup cooked or canned navy or cannellini beans, drained and rinsed

2 tablespoons freshly squeezed lemon juice

1 tablespoon apple cider vinegar

¼ cup dehydrated minced onion

1¼ teaspoons onion powder

2 teaspoons nutritional yeast

1 teaspoon sea salt or to taste

½–¾ cup water or aquafaba

Optional Garnishes
Roasted onion, fresh herbs, cashews

Preparation

1. Drain the cashews, discard the soaking liquid, and add the drained cashews, beans, lemon juice, apple cider vinegar, minced onion, onion powder, nutritional yeast, salt, and ½ cup of water or aquafaba to a high-speed blender. Blend on high for 30 to 60 seconds, using your tamper to assist the blending, until the mix is completely smooth. It will be stiff, like a cream cheese, which is how I like it. Add more water as needed to reach a looser, dip-like texture if desired.

2. Transfer to a serving bowl, garnish with roasted onions, fresh herbs or cashews, and serve. Add a dollop of this to any salad, soup, or warm grain dish for an instant upgrade!

Brilliant Beet Hummus

That pop of brilliant hot pink is hard to resist! Roasted sweet beets are the star of this hummus. Try layering it with avocado on whole-grain bread or on toasted Mini Buckwheat Bagels (page 75). Divine!

Makes 3 cups

Ingredients

1 small or medium red beet, chopped, roasted, and cooled (see Roasting Beets below) (½ heaping cup)

2 cups cooked or canned chickpeas, drained and rinsed

3 garlic cloves

2 tablespoons well-stirred tahini

3 tablespoons freshly squeezed lemon juice

⅛ teaspoon cayenne pepper

½ teaspoon sea salt or to taste

2–6 tablespoons water or aquafaba

Preparation

1. Place the roasted beet, chickpeas, garlic, tahini, lemon juice, cayenne, and salt in a food processor and process continuously. Add water or aquafaba, gradually, as you process until a creamy consistency is reached. Taste and reseason.

Variations: Try adding a couple of teaspoons of balsamic vinegar, using almond butter instead of tahini, or roasted garlic instead of raw.

Roasting Beets

You can find pre-roasted beets packed in water or vacuum packed in many grocery stores, but you can easily roast them at home. Simply scrub the beets, cut them into quarters, and place in an oven safe dish and cover. Roast beets in an oven preheated to 425°F for 40 to 60 minutes until they're easily pierced with a fork. Set aside to cool. Once cooled, peel, and they're ready to use. You can keep roasted beets in the fridge in a sealed container for up to 5 days.

Herbed Cheeze Ball

I take every opportunity to share plant-based meals and recipes, especially at big gatherings over the holidays. It's always a conversation starter and inevitably leads to "wait, this is vegan? NO!" This cheese-inspired nut ball is my tried-and-tested version of a classic crowd-pleaser. It's pretty much legendary! It's important to soak the cashews and walnuts ahead of time to help with digestion and to make them easier to mold into a ball.

Makes 1 large or 2 medium cheeze balls

Ingredients

1 cup whole cashews

1 cup whole walnuts

2 tablespoons white miso

2 tablespoons nutritional yeast

2 tablespoons freshly squeezed lemon juice

2 teaspoons dried basil

1 teaspoon dehydrated minced onion

1 teaspoon dried oregano

½ teaspoon onion powder

¼ teaspoon red pepper flakes, optional

Optional Garnishes for Rolling/Coating

1 small bunch parsley or chives, finely chopped

3 tablespoons dehydrated minced onion

¼ cup finely diced red bell pepper

1 tablespoon red pepper flakes (reduce/omit for a
   less spicy version)

Variations: You can make this into different-size cheeze balls as well. Try serving personal-sized cheeze balls (a few tablespoons each) as an appetizer or make two medium-sized balls and freeze one for later. You can also crumble this cheeze ball into a salad or hot pasta for an extra punch of delicious flavor!

Preparation

1. Soak the cashews and walnuts in the same bowl of water for 4 hours. The nuts will darken in color while soaking; that's okay.

2. Drain the nuts, discard the soaking liquid, and add the drained nuts to a food processor with all other ingredients (except the garnishes). Process until all the ingredients are well combined and the mixture comes together and starts rolling around the processor in a ball. Scrape the sides and bottom of the container a couple of times throughout to incorporate all ingredients.

3. Remove the mixture from the food processor, shape into a ball with your hands, and transfer to a bowl. Cover and let the ball sit in the fridge for 12 to 24 hours (not absolutely essential, but this allows the flavors to deepen and the ball to set). I like to place a little piece of parchment paper in the bottom of the bowl to prevent sticking.

4. When ready to serve, mix the rolling/coating ingredients together on a large plate or piece of parchment paper. Remove the ball from the fridge and with damp hands reshape the ball and gently roll in the coating mixture. Serve with whole-grain crackers.

PLANTIFUL PLATES & BOWLS

REINVENTING DINNER

From working with and making meals for people of all ages and backgrounds, I've learned that the entree or dinner can be a challenge when it comes to planning, variety, and presentation on a plant-based diet (especially at first).

I invite you to take this opportunity to reinvent your plate and bowl and let go of the old notion that dinner is a "main" protein and a combination of side dishes. In this chapter you'll find familiar recipes like pasta, burgers, casseroles, and sheet-pan dinners as well as others that might have unfamiliar names or flavor combinations.

Try them all because you never know what might become your new favorite!

The Parmesans   149

Tuesday Tempeh Tacos   151

Cauliflower Potato Dal   152

Rustic Mashed Potatoes & Mushroom-Miso Gravy   155

Portobello Pizzas with Sunflower Mozzarella   157

Chickpea Smash Lettuce Cups   161

Vegetable Jambalaya   162

Chinese "Fried" Quinoa   165

Building a Bowl   167

Golden Bowls   169

Fresh Falafel & Tzatziki Bowl   171

Balsamic Tempeh & Brussels Sprouts Bowl   175

Pink Quinoa & Cheezy Kale Bowl   176

Fiesta Burrito Bowls   179

BBQ Sheet-Pan Dinner   180

Sweet & Sour Chickpea-Stuffed Sweet Potatoes   183

The Blackout Burger   185

B's Burger   189

Creamy Romesco & Roasted Cauliflower Penne   191

Red Lentil Marinara Spaghetti   195

Perfect Green-Pea Pesto Pasta   197

Market Shepherd's Pie   199

Vegetable Lasagna & Tofu Ricotta with House Marinara   201

One-Pot Broccoli Hummus Mac n' Cheeze   207

Weeknight Tempeh & Vegetable Casserole   209

The Parmesans

Not a main meal but rather a seasoning that we cannot live without! I have at least one of these Parmesans in my fridge at all times. They only take a few minutes to make and just a teaspoon or two can completely transform any plant-based dinner! I use these as garnishes or ingredients throughout this book. The nuts aren't soaked for this recipe.

Classic Almond Parmesan

A classic Parmesan-inspired seasoning that pairs well with anything!

Ingredients

1 cup almonds
¼ cup nutritional yeast flakes
2 teaspoons dried thyme
1 teaspoon dried oregano
1 teaspoon sea salt

Hickory Almond Parmesan

This is a smoky, mildly spicy seasoning that adds a flavorful kick to pastas, pizzas, grain dishes, and soups.

Ingredients

1 cup almonds
3 tablespoons nutritional yeast flakes
1½ teaspoons smoked paprika
1 teaspoon red pepper flakes
¾ teaspoons sea salt

Cashew Turmeric Parmesan

An anti-inflammatory Parmesan with an extra cheezy flavor! This one is a household favorite.

Ingredients

1 cup cashews
3 tablespoons nutritional yeast flakes
2 tablespoons white sesame seeds
1¼ teaspoons ground turmeric
1 teaspoon sea salt
¼ teaspoon black pepper

Preparation

1. The preparation is the same for each recipe. Add all the chosen Parmesan ingredients to a food processor in the order listed and process continuously until the nuts are a fine, sandy texture. Stop and scrape down the sides and bottom of the food processor 2 or 3 times throughout. Be careful not to overprocess, or you'll end up with nut butter! Transfer the Parmesan to a glass jar with a lid and keep in the fridge for up to a month.

Variations: Try replacing ¼ to ½ cup nuts with an equivalent amount of hemp seeds for a slightly different flavor and nutritional boost!

Tuesday Tempeh Tacos

Yeah, we do taco night! I wasn't trying to imitate the classic taco, but I have to admit that these tacos taste like the original. Tempeh mixed with spices and salsa makes for a chunky, hearty, and flavorful filling. Easy to make and you can use whatever taco shell you like—corn or brown rice tortilla or sturdy lettuce leaves. Serve these with a side salad or Tahini Caesar (page 113) for the best #tacotuesday ever!

Makes 4 servings

Ingredients

1 (8 ounce) package tempeh

½ yellow or red onion, diced

4 ounces button or cremini mushrooms, chopped

1 red bell pepper, deseeded and diced

1 small jalapeño, deseeded and diced (omit for less spicy option)

2½ teaspoons chili powder

2 teaspoons ground cumin

1 teaspoon garlic powder

½ teaspoon dried oregano

½ teaspoon smoked paprika

1 tablespoon tamari

½ cup chunky salsa (your favorite!)

1 lime, cut into wedges

8–10 corn tortillas (warmed)

1 head Boston lettuce (if using tortillas)

1–2 avocados, pits removed, peeled and chopped or Avocado Tartare (page 131) or Sour Cream (page 97)

Optional Garnish
Chopped cilantro or parsley

Preparation

1. Break the tempeh into 2 to 3 pieces. Place in a food processor and pulse until crumbly. Alternatively, finely chop the tempeh. Set aside.

2. In a large sauté pan, sauté the onion in a few tablespoons of water for 5 minutes until translucent.

3. Add the mushrooms, red pepper, jalapeño, crumbled tempeh, and all the spices and continue to cook on medium heat for another 6 to 8 minutes until the tempeh and mushrooms begin to brown. Stir often and add water as needed, 1 to 2 tablespoons at a time, to prevent burning.

4. Now, add the tamari and salsa and continue to simmer for another 6 to 8 minutes. The taco "meat" should be thick and chunky. Add a squeeze of lime juice, taste, and reseason.

5. If using corn tortillas, first add a layer of lettuce leaves (this helps keep the tacos from getting soggy), then fill with taco meat. Top with avocado, Avocado Tartare or Sour Cream, and cilantro and serve with a slice of lime.

Recipe Recycle: Serve the tempeh filling on top of baked potatoes with Sour Cream (page 97).

Cauliflower Potato Dal

Indian cuisine has taught me so much about herbs and spices and flavor! If you're not familiar with vegan Indian cuisine, I highly recommend the Vegan Richa's Indian Kitchen *cookbook. One dish I learned early in my plant-based journey was dal. Dal refers to dried legumes like lentils and peas and dishes made from these legumes. They're easy and filling and budget-friendly. This dal made with split red lentils (masoor dal), fragrant spices, and flavor-building veggies is simply delicious! Red lentils cook quickly and don't require soaking. Pair this with cooked brown rice or enjoy on its own.*

Makes 4–6 servings

Ingredients

1 medium red onion, diced

5 garlic cloves, minced

1 tablespoon garam masala

1 tablespoon ground cumin

2 teaspoons ground coriander

1 teaspoon ground fenugreek

½ teaspoon ground turmeric

¼ teaspoon red pepper flakes or to your preference

2 red potatoes, peel on, chopped into 1-inch cubes

1¼ cups split red lentils, rinsed

4 cups low-sodium vegetable broth

1 (14.5-ounce) can diced tomatoes

2 tablespoons tomato paste

4 cups bite-sized cauliflower florets (1 small head cauliflower)

2 teaspoons freshly squeezed lemon juice

2 cups baby spinach or chopped kale

½ teaspoon sea salt or to taste

Black pepper

Preparation

1. In a large sauté pan, sauté the red onion with a few tablespoons of water for 5 to 7 minutes or until the onions become translucent. Add water as needed to prevent burning.

2. Add the garlic, spices, and potatoes. Stir to coat everything in spices and continue to sauté for another 2 minutes, adding water as needed.

3. Add the lentils, vegetable broth, diced tomatoes, and tomato paste and stir. Bring to a boil, then reduce to a simmer, partially cover, and simmer for 15 minutes, stirring occasionally. Now, add the cauliflower and continue to simmer, covered, for another 10 minutes.

4. Remove the cover and cook for another 5 minutes or until the veggies are tender and the lentils have absorbed most of the broth.

5. Finally, add the lemon juice, greens, and salt. Stir and remove from heat. The greens will wilt quickly. Taste and reseason with salt and pepper and serve.

Rustic Mashed Potatoes & Mushroom-Miso Gravy

Potatoes are my definition of comfort food but they're also health supportive, offering fiber, B vitamins, and potassium. I like them cooked any way, but this recipe is a complete meal! Beans are mashed right in and then topped with miso gravy. Add greens for a pop of color and phytonutrients. Leaving the peel on the potato gives the dish a more "rustic" feel. The gravy also freezes well—I often make a double batch and freeze half.

Makes 4 servings

Ingredients

Rustic Mashed Potatoes

5 medium Yukon Gold potatoes, peel on, roughly chopped

1½ cups cooked or canned navy beans, drained and rinsed

2 tablespoons Dijon mustard

2 tablespoons nutritional yeast

½ teaspoons garlic powder

¼–½ cup unsweetened soy or almond milk

½ teaspoon sea salt or to taste

2 cups baby spinach or arugula, optional

Mushroom Gravy

½ cup finely diced shallot or yellow onion

5 garlic cloves, minced

6 ounces button or cremini mushrooms, thinly sliced

1 teaspoon dried thyme or 1 heaping tablespoon fresh thyme

¼ teaspoon red pepper flakes or to your preference

2 cups low-sodium vegetable broth, separated

2 tablespoons nutritional yeast

2 tablespoons tamari

2 teaspoons balsamic vinegar

1 teaspoon red wine vinegar

1 tablespoon + 2 teaspoons white miso

2 tablespoons arrowroot starch

Black pepper

Preparation

1. Place the potatoes in a pot of cold salted water and bring to a boil. Once boiling, reduce to a simmer and simmer uncovered for 10 to 15 minutes or until the potatoes are tender. Add the beans to the pot for the last few minutes of cooking.

2. Drain the potatoes and beans and return them to the pot. Add the Dijon mustard, nutritional yeast, garlic powder, salt, and ¼ cup of milk and mash well with a potato masher. Add more milk as needed to get a creamy texture. Mash in the greens if using. Taste and reseason and cover.

3. While the potatoes are cooking, make the gravy. Add the shallot or onion to a medium pot and sauté in a few tablespoons of water until translucent, about 5 to 7 minutes, adding water as needed. Now, add the garlic, sliced mushrooms, thyme, and red pepper flakes and continue to cook on medium heat for 5 minutes, stirring often, until the mushrooms shrink and release their juices.

4. Next, to a blender add 1½ cups broth, nutritional yeast, tamari, balsamic and red wine vinegars, and miso and blend until

(Continued on next page)

smooth. Pour this mixture into the pot with the sautéed onions and mushrooms and bring to a simmer. Simmer uncovered on low to medium heat for 5 minutes, then reduce the heat to low.

5. Mix the remaining ½ cup vegetable broth and arrowroot starch together in a bowl until the arrowroot is dissolved. Add this to the pot of gravy, stir, and simmer on low heat for another minute; the gravy should thicken quickly. Season with pepper.

6. Divide the potatoes among bowls and top with gravy.

Portobello Pizzas
with Sunflower Mozzarella

Here portobello mushrooms are stuffed with a "cheese" made from sunflower seeds and cashews then topped with sautéed onion, tomatoes, and capers. You can serve these on their own or with warm quinoa or a side salad. The sunflower seeds and cashews need to be soaked ahead of time and can be soaked in the same bowl. Final yield will depend on the size of the mushrooms.

Makes 8–10 Portobello Pizzas (depending on size)

Ingredients

Sunflower Mozzarella

½ cup cashews, soaked for 3 hours

1½ cups sunflower seeds, soaked for 3 hours

3 garlic cloves, minced

¼ cup freshly squeezed lemon juice

¾ teaspoon dried basil

½ teaspoon dried oregano

¾ teaspoon sea salt

½ cup water

Mushrooms

8–10 portobello mushrooms, stems removed and reserved

1 tablespoon tamari

1 tablespoon balsamic vinegar

2 heaping cups thinly sliced red or yellow onion

Generous pinch of salt

3 garlic cloves, minced

½ teaspoon dried basil

½ teaspoon dried oregano

2 heaping cups cherry tomatoes, sliced

3 tablespoons capers, drained and roughly chopped

Handful fresh basil leaves or baby arugula

Preparation

1. Position the oven rack to the middle of the oven and preheat to 350°F. Line a large baking sheet with parchment paper.

2. First, make the mozzarella. Drain the cashews and sunflower seeds, discard the soaking liquid, and transfer the drained nuts and seeds to a high-speed blender. Add the garlic, lemon juice, basil, oregano, salt, and ½ cup water. Blend on high until smooth using your tamper to assist the blending. The goal is to achieve a thick but smooth and spreadable texture. Set aside.

3. Wipe the mushrooms clean and gently remove the stems. Finely chop the stems and set aside.

4. In a small bowl mix together the tamari and balsamic vinegar. Then, using a basting brush or your hands, rub the mixture into the tops (caps) of the mushrooms. Place the mushrooms top-side down on the baking sheet so the inside of the mushroom is facing up.

5. Spoon 2 to 4 tablespoons of sunflower mozzarella (depending on the size of mushrooms) into each cap and spread it

(Continued on page 159)

Variations: For a nut-free version, swap another ½ cup sunflower seeds for the cashews.

Recipe Recycle: Spread leftover Sunflower Mozzarella on toasted bread or add a spoonful to a hot baked potato or warm pasta. We love to add a smear to B's Burger (page 189).

evenly. Place the mushrooms in the oven and bake for 17 to 20 minutes, or until the mushrooms just start to release their juices but are still firm.

6. Meanwhile, in a large nonstick sauté pan, sauté the onion with about ¼ cup water and a generous pinch of salt for 10 minutes, stirring occasionally and adding water as needed, until the onions start to caramelize. Add the finely chopped mushroom stems, garlic, basil, oregano, and tomatoes to the pan and continue to cook over medium heat for another 5 minutes until the tomatoes start to brown and any liquid in the pan evaporates. Add the capers, stir, and remove from heat.

7. Once the mushroom caps are done, remove from the oven and spoon the onion/tomato mix onto each mushroom. Top with fresh basil or arugula and serve.

Chickpea Smash Lettuce Cups

A super easy recipe that you can make in less than 15 minutes! Crisp lettuce serves as a vehicle for the tangy, creamy, and crunchy chickpea avocado smash. You can serve this for lunch or a light dinner.

Makes 2–4 servings

Ingredients

1½ cups cooked or canned chickpeas, drained and
    rinsed

1 ripe avocado, pit removed, peeled

1 teaspoon Dijon mustard

1 tablespoon freshly squeezed lemon juice

1 garlic clove, minced

¼ heaping cup finely diced red bell pepper

¼ heaping cup thinly sliced celery

¼ heaping cup finely diced dill pickles

1 scallion, thinly sliced

¼ teaspoon sea salt

8 romaine lettuce leaves

Optional Additions

¼ cup raisins, dried cranberries, diced apple, diced
    cucumber, sliced olives

Optional Garnishes

Sliced cherry tomatoes, sprouts, scallions

Preparation

1. Add the chickpeas to a large bowl and mash with a fork or potato masher until most of the chickpeas are broken up. You can leave some whole for extra texture.

2. Add the avocado, mustard, lemon juice, and garlic and mash again until well incorporated. Add the red pepper, celery, pickles, scallion, and salt and mix again. Taste and reseason if needed. Scoop ¼ cup of the mix into each romaine leaf and garnish with sliced tomatoes, sprouts, and/or additional scallions.

Recipe Recycle: Add a scoop of this chickpea smash to salads or serve it in a brown rice wrap or on sprouted bread as a sandwich.

Vegetable Jambalaya

Jambalaya is a Louisiana rice dish that's big on flavor thanks to an incredible combination of herbs and spices. This vegan version is a one-pot recipe that I return to often. It's easy to put together and is even better leftover! I like to serve this alone or with additional steamed veggies.

Makes 4–6 servings

Ingredients

1 large yellow onion, diced

2 large celery stalks, thinly sliced

2 medium carrots, diced

4 garlic cloves, minced

1 red bell pepper, deseeded and diced

1½ teaspoon dried oregano

1½ teaspoon smoked paprika

1 teaspoon dried thyme

1 teaspoon onion powder

1 teaspoon garlic powder

¼ teaspoon red pepper flakes or to your preference

2 bay leaves

1 (14.5-ounce) can diced tomatoes (regular or fire-roasted)

3 cups low-sodium vegetable broth (more if needed)

1¼ cups long-grain brown rice

1 cup frozen peas

1 tablespoon tamari

1 cup baby spinach or chopped kale

Sea salt and black pepper

Optional Garnish
Parsley

Preparation

1. In a large pot, sauté the onion, celery, and carrots with about ¼ cup water for 7 to 10 minutes, or until the onion is translucent and the carrots have softened. Add water as needed to prevent burning.

2. Add the garlic, bell pepper, and all the spices and continue to cook on medium heat for another 2 minutes, stirring often.

3. Add the bay leaves, diced tomatoes, vegetable broth, and brown rice. Cover the pot and bring to a boil. Once boiling reduce to a simmer and simmer covered for 55 minutes. Check the rice around the 40-minute mark. If there's no broth remaining, stir in another ¼ to ½ cup, cover, and continue cooking. Check a few times during the final 10 minutes to make sure the rice isn't sticking to the pot. When the rice is tender and all the liquid is absorbed, remove from heat, and let sit covered for 5 minutes.

4. Remove the bay leaves and finish the jambalaya by adding the green peas, tamari, and spinach or kale. Stir and leave covered for another few minutes until the greens wilt. Taste and reseason with salt and pepper. Divide among bowls and garnish with parsley.

Chinese "Fried" Quinoa

This was inspired by traditional fried rice but includes some healthy twists—quinoa instead of rice, tofu instead of egg, and "fried" without oil. This recipe calls for black salt, or kala namak, for an egg-y aroma and taste (page 23). It's not necessary but intensifies the flavor! Serve this on its own or with steamed broccoli.

Makes 4 servings

Ingredients

1 cup dry white quinoa

1 large yellow onion, finely diced

3 cloves garlic, minced

1 red or orange bell pepper, deseeded and diced

1 stalk celery, thinly sliced

6 ounces cremini or shiitake mushrooms, thinly sliced

1 (12–14 ounce) block extra-firm organic tofu

½ teaspoon ground turmeric

¼ teaspoon red pepper flakes or to your preference

¾ teaspoon Indian black salt (kala namak)

Pinch black pepper

2 tablespoons tamari or to taste

1 cup frozen green peas

1 cup finely chopped spinach or kale

3 scallions, thinly sliced

3 tablespoons sesame seeds

Preparation

1. Rinse the quinoa in a fine-mesh strainer and cook according to package directions. Once cooked, fluff with a fork, cover, and set aside.

2. While the quinoa is cooking, add the diced onion to a large nonstick sauté pan and sauté in a few tablespoons of water until translucent, 5 to 7 minutes. Add more water as needed to prevent burning.

3. Now, add the garlic, bell pepper, celery, and mushrooms and continue to sauté on medium heat for another 5 minutes until the mushrooms begin releasing their juices.

4. Reduce the heat to low. Drain the tofu and squeeze it above a bowl or sink to remove the excess liquid, then, using your hands, crumble it into small pieces into the pan. Add the turmeric, red pepper flakes, black salt, and black pepper, and stir. Raise the heat to medium and cook the tofu for about 5 minutes, stirring frequently, or until the tofu starts to brown and any liquid in the pan has evaporated.

5. Then, add the cooked quinoa and stir. Add tamari, frozen green peas, and chopped spinach or kale, and mix. Cook on medium heat for another minute until the greens are bright green. Taste and reseason with tamari if needed. Divide among bowls and garnish with scallions and sesame seeds.

BUILDING A BOWL

We just call them bowls! "Bowls" is pretty much shorthand for a one-bowl meal made from whole grains, vibrant veggies, plant-based protein, and a host of endless extras. Also known as *nourish* or *power* bowls, this meal is a template for a wholesome, nutritionally balanced meal where you can easily swap or alter ingredients according to what you have on hand or what's in season. The picture on the cover of this book is actually a random combination of what I had in my fridge including roasted cauliflower from the Golden Bowls (page 169), Fresh Falafel (page 171), and Tahini Caesar with Quick Smoked Chickpeas and Bacon-ish Bits (page 113) recipes.

We have some form of a bowl at least three nights a week—mostly for convenience, as it's a great way to repurpose leftovers. Also inherent in the notion of a bowl is arranging the different components in sections and including colorful produce. Here's how I build mine:

- **Whole grains:** the foundation of any bowl. I like to use warm quinoa or brown rice.
- **Plant-based protein:** This can be in the form of hummus, leftover burgers, bean balls, baked tempeh or tofu, or cooked legumes. I usually start planning my bowl with this component. It's where you can introduce some unexpected flavor and texture.
- **Vibrant veggies:** I like to add a mix of raw and cooked veggies using a variety of cooking methods to switch it up.
- **Sauce:** The hero of a bowl! A good sauce can transform any ho-hum meal into a five-star experience. This is where I introduce healthy fats in the form of nuts or seeds or their butters.
- **Fun extras:** Anything from fresh herbs, microgreens, avocado, nuts, seeds, or seaweeds can be used as a garnish to add a pop of flavor, crunch, and nutrition!

Golden Bowls

After reading Building a Bowl (page 167) you know how flexible this meal is! This bowl is one I make with a creamy anti-inflammatory turmeric sauce and turmeric-roasted cauliflower, hence "golden." In this bowl, the protein component can be anything you like—reheat frozen B's Burgers (page 189), a scoop of Spiced Creamy Carrot Hummus (page 139), or Balsamic Tempeh (page 175).

Makes 3 servings

Ingredients

Bowl

1 cup dry white quinoa or brown rice

¾ teaspoon each ground turmeric, coriander, garlic powder

4 grinds black pepper

6 cups bite-sized cauliflower florets (1 medium-large head cauliflower)

Plant-based protein of choice (in this picture, 3 B's Burger, cut in half)

1 bunch curly kale, stems removed, chopped (5 packed cups)

½ lemon

1½ cups cherry tomatoes, halved

¼ cup raw or toasted pumpkin seeds

Golden Tahini Sauce

¼ cup well-stirred tahini

2 tablespoons freshly squeezed lemon juice

1 garlic clove, minced

2 teaspoon maple syrup, optional

1 teaspoon nutritional yeast

¼ teaspoon ground turmeric

⅛ teaspoon cayenne pepper

Pinch black pepper

2 tablespoons water

Preparation

1. First, make the grains according to package directions. Once cooked, fluff with a fork, cover, and set aside.

2. Meanwhile, preheat the oven to 425°F and line a baking sheet with parchment paper. In a small bowl, mix together the turmeric, coriander, garlic powder, and black pepper.

3. Place the cauliflower florets in a large bowl. Sprinkle half the spice mix over the cauliflower and toss to combine. Sprinkle the remaining spice mix and toss again ensuring all florets are coated in spices. Transfer the cauliflower to the baking sheet and bake for 30 to 35 minutes, flipping halfway through, until the cauliflower is tender and the edges of the florets begin to brown.

4. Make the sauce by whisking all the ingredients together in a small bowl until smooth. Add more water, 1 tablespoon at a time, to reach a smooth, pourable consistency.

5. If using burgers or falafel that need reheating, add them to the pan of cauliflower for the last 10 minutes. When the cauliflower is almost done, add the kale to a large sauté pan and sauté with a few tablespoons of

(Continued on next page)

Turmeric

Turmeric and one of its primary active phytonutrients, curcumin, have earned nutritional notoriety. Numerous studies have proven that turmeric has serious, head-turning anti-inflammatory properties. Combining turmeric with black pepper improves its absorption, so use them together whenever possible!

water, stirring, for a couple of minutes until bright green and wilting. Add a squeeze of lemon and pinch of salt.

6. Assemble the bowls by dividing the grains, cauliflower, plant-based protein of choice, kale, and tomatoes between bowls. Garnish with pumpkin seeds and drizzle with Golden Tahini Sauce.

Fresh Falafel & Tzatziki Bowl

I keep these falafels on hand for a quick snack, to add to salads, and for this fresh Mediterranean-inspired bowl. I suggest you either make the tzatziki ahead of time or whip it up while the falafel and quinoa are cooking. Use leftover tzatziki as a veggie dip, in a wrap, or add a dollop to warm grains and steamed veg!

Makes 4 bowls or 26–30 falafel balls

Ingredients

Chickpea Falafel

3 tablespoons ground flax seeds

6 tablespoons water

1 medium carrot, roughly chopped (1 heaping cup)

½ cup walnuts

3 cups cooked or canned chickpeas, drained and rinsed

½ cup gluten-free oat flour

3 tablespoons nutritional yeast

2 teaspoons garlic powder

1 teaspoon onion powder

¼ teaspoon red pepper flakes or to your preference

2 tablespoons freshly squeezed lemon juice

¾ teaspoon sea salt

Tzatziki

1 cup cashews, soaked for 2–3 hours

3 tablespoons freshly squeezed lemon juice

1 garlic clove

2 teaspoons maple syrup

1 tablespoon nutritional yeast

¾ teaspoon onion powder

¾ teaspoon sea salt

½ cup water

1 teaspoon dried dill or 1 tablespoon fresh dill

½ cup grated cucumber, peel on

Bowl

1 cup dry white quinoa

2 zucchini, peeled into ribbons or spiralized

6–8 Campari tomatoes, quartered or 2 cups cherry tomatoes, halved

4 cups arugula

(Continued on page 173)

Preparation

1. First, make the falafel. Position the oven rack in the middle of the oven and preheat to 350°F. Line a baking sheet with parchment paper.

2. Place the ground flax seeds in a small bowl and add 6 tablespoons of water. Mix and set aside for 5 minutes to thicken.

3. Add the chopped carrot to a food processor and process briefly until shredded, then transfer to a large bowl.

4. Next, add the walnuts to the food processor and pulse a few times until the walnuts are broken up into a crumbly texture. Transfer the walnuts to the bowl with the carrots.

5. Now add the chickpeas, oat flour, nutritional yeast, garlic powder, onion powder, red pepper flakes, lemon juice, salt, and the flax mixture to the food processor and process briefly until the mixture is well combined and the chickpeas are no longer whole. Stop and scrape down the sides once or twice and pulse to incorporate all ingredients.

6. Transfer the chickpea mixture to the bowl with the carrots and walnuts and mix well until everything is combined.

7. With damp hands, scoop out about 2 tablespoons of the mix and roll into a ball and place on the baking sheet. I like to use a ¾-ounce spring-release scoop or disher to scoop and shape the balls (see page 11). Repeat with remaining falafel mixture. You should get between 26 and 30 falafels.

8. Bake in the oven for 50 to 55 minutes, gently flipping halfway through. They're done when browned and firm to the touch. Remove from the oven and let rest for 5 minutes before serving; they'll continue to firm as they cool.

9. While the falafel is baking, rinse and cook the quinoa according to package directions, prepare the vegetables, and make the tzatziki as follows. Drain the cashews, discard the soaking liquid, and add the drained cashews, lemon juice, garlic, maple syrup, nutritional yeast, onion powder, salt, and water to a high-speed blender. Blend on high until completely smooth. Add the dill and blend briefly just to combine.

10. Transfer the tzatziki to a bowl. Gently squeeze out and discard any extra liquid in the grated cucumber—it doesn't need to be completely dry—and mix into the tzatziki.

11. Divide the falafel, quinoa, and veggies between bowls and serve with tzatziki. Keep leftover falafel or tzatziki in the fridge for 3 days or freeze the falafel for up to 3 months.

Variations: Substitute raw beet for the carrots or cannellini beans for the chickpeas in the falafel.

Balsamic Tempeh & Brussels Sprouts Bowl

This is a beautiful, balanced bowl with four easy components: marinated tempeh, herbed rice, steamed veggies, and creamy sauce. The cashews and dates need to be soaked ahead of time.

Makes 3–4 servings

Ingredients

Tempeh Marinade

1 (8-ounce) package tempeh, diced into ¾-inch cubes

¼ cup balsamic vinegar

2 tablespoons tamari

2 teaspoons maple syrup, optional

2 garlic cloves, minced

¼ teaspoon red pepper flakes or to your preference

Herbed Rice

1½ cups dry long-grain brown rice

2 heaping tablespoons each chopped fresh rosemary and thyme leaves, optional

Date & Dijon Sauce

¼ cup cashews, soaked in water for 2–3 hours

3 pitted Medjool dates, soaked in hot water for 15–30 minutes

3 tablespoons smooth Dijon mustard (not grainy)

2 tablespoons apple cider vinegar

1 small garlic clove

¼ teaspoon sea salt

2 pinches black pepper

Scant ½ cup water

Veggies

4 cups brussels sprouts, trimmed and halved

Variations: Try using broccoli instead of brussels sprouts or Tahini Dill Sauce (page 183) instead of Date and Dijon.

Preparation

1. Place the diced tempeh and all marinade ingredients in a container (ideally with a lid). Flip the container back and forth to coat the tempeh and let marinate for 20 minutes, flipping a few times throughout.

2. While the tempeh is marinating, cook the rice according to package directions. Once cooked, fluff with a fork, fold in fresh herbs, cover, and set aside.

3. Next, make the sauce. Drain the dates and cashews, discard the soaking liquid, and add the drained dates and cashews along with all sauce ingredients to a high-speed blender and blend on high until smooth. Add more water, 1 tablespoon at a time, if needed to reach smooth, pourable consistency.

4. Transfer the tempeh and the marinade to a nonstick sauté pan and cook over medium heat for 5 minutes or until the tempeh is browned and the marinade has evaporated. Stir occasionally and add water as needed to prevent burning or sticking. Remove from heat and cover to keep warm.

5. Finally, steam the brussels sprouts in a pot fitted with a steamer basket until the sprouts are bright green and tender, this will depend on how big your sprouts are.

6. Divide the rice, brussels sprouts, and tempeh between bowls and drizzle with creamy sauce!

Pink Quinoa & Cheezy Kale Bowl

This anti-inflammatory and protein-packed dish has two parts—pink quinoa made in a pot and cheezy kale and chickpeas made in a sauté pan. It's ideal to have the Cashew Turmeric Parmesan made ahead of time (even better to always have it on hand). Also, a reminder to use the appropriately sized pot (1½ to 2 quart) for the quinoa; too large a pot and the quinoa won't cook properly. The cheezy kale also makes an easy side dish that pairs well with almost anything.

Makes 3 servings

Ingredients

Pink Quinoa

¾ cup dry white quinoa

1 tablespoon nutritional yeast

2 teaspoons ground coriander

1½ teaspoons sweet paprika

¾ teaspoon cinnamon

1 cup finely diced raw red beet

1 tablespoon tamari

2 teaspoons balsamic vinegar

1¾ cups water

Cheezy Kale

1 medium red onion, thinly sliced

¼ teaspoon red pepper flakes or to your
   preference

¼ teaspoon cinnamon

Pinch sea salt

1½ cups cooked or canned chickpeas, drained and
   rinsed

1 bunch lacinato or curly kale, stems removed,
   chopped (5 packed cups)

1 tablespoon freshly squeezed lemon juice

¼ cup Cashew Turmeric Parmesan (page 149),
   plus more for serving

Variations: Try any of the Parmesans (page 149) for this recipe.

Preparation

1. Rinse the quinoa in a fine-mesh strainer and transfer to a 1½ to 2-quart saucepan with the nutritional yeast, coriander, paprika, and cinnamon. Cook for 30 seconds over medium heat, stirring, until the spices are fragrant. Now, add the diced beet, tamari, balsamic vinegar, and water. Cover, bring to a boil, then reduce to a gentle simmer. Simmer for 16 to 18 minutes or until the quinoa has absorbed all the water. Avoid removing the cover before the 15-minute mark. Once cooked, remove the cover and fluff with a fork and scrape the bottom of the pot to mix in any beets that have sunk to the bottom. Quickly cover and set aside to continue steaming.

2. While the quinoa is continuing to steam, make the cheezy kale. Add the red onion to a large sauté pan and sauté with a few tablespoons of water for 5 minutes. Add water as needed to prevent burning.

3. Next, add the red pepper flakes, cinnamon, salt, chickpeas, and kale. Stir and continue to cook for another few minutes until heated throughout and the kale begins to wilt. Finally, stir in the lemon juice and ¼ cup Cashew Turmeric Parmesan.

4. To serve, divide the quinoa and kale between bowls and garnish with an extra sprinkle of Parmesan.

Fiesta Burrito Bowls

A Mexican-inspired bowl of goodness! This layered dish is like a deconstructed burrito, all the fixings together in a bowl instead of a wrap! It's easy to make and is extra delicious with a dollop of Sour Cream (page 97)—a highly recommended addition!

Makes 3–4 servings

Ingredients

1½ cups dry brown rice

1 large red onion, diced

4 garlic cloves, minced

1 small jalapeño, deseeded and diced

1 red bell pepper, deseeded and diced

1 yellow bell pepper, deseeded and diced

1 tablespoon chili powder

1 teaspoon ground cumin

1 teaspoon sweet paprika

1 teaspoon dried oregano

½ teaspoon garlic powder

½ teaspoon onion powder

1 (14.5 ounce) can diced tomatoes (regular or fire roasted)

1 cup frozen corn kernels

1½ cups cooked or canned black beans, drained and rinsed

1 packed cup finely chopped kale or baby spinach

1 tablespoon freshly squeezed lime juice

½ teaspoon sea salt or to taste

1 batch Sour Cream (page 97)

1 avocado, pit removed, peeled, and thinly sliced

3 scallions, thinly sliced

Optional Garnishes
1 small bunch cilantro, sliced scallions, lime wedges

Preparation

1. Cook the rice according to package directions. Once cooked, fluff with a fork, cover, and set aside.

2. Meanwhile, in a large sauté pan, sauté the onion in about ¼ cup water for 7 to 10 minutes, or until the onions have softened. Add the garlic, jalapeño, bell peppers, and all spices and continue to sauté for another 3 minutes, stirring often, and adding water as needed to prevent burning.

3. Now, add the diced tomatoes, frozen corn, and black beans and simmer uncovered, stirring often, for 7 to 10 minutes or until most of the liquid from the tomatoes has evaporated. Add the kale or spinach and cook for another minute until bright green and wilted. Finally, add the lime juice and salt to taste. Layer each bowl with rice, tomato/bean mix, a dollop of Sour Cream (page 97), and sliced avocado. Garnish with cilantro, scallions, and a lime wedge.

BBQ Sheet-Pan Dinner

I love a good sheet-pan dinner! Here halfway way through baking, the veggies are tossed with a refined-sugar-free BBQ sauce and baked again. If you like your veggies with a crunch, shorten the baking time. This can be served as a dish on its own, on top of cooked quinoa, or with a side of steamed greens. You can also make the sauce ahead of time for easy weeknight cleanup (it freezes well too).

Makes 4 servings

Ingredients

1 large red onion, chopped into 1-inch pieces

1 medium Yukon Gold potato, peel on, chopped into 1-inch cubes

1 medium sweet potato, peel on, chopped into 1-inch cubes

1 red bell pepper, deseeded and chopped into 1-inch pieces

5 cups bite-sized cauliflower florets (1 medium head cauliflower)

1½ cups cooked or canned chickpeas, drained and rinsed

BBQ Sauce

½ cup packed pitted soft Medjool or Deglet Nour dates*

¼ cup tomato paste

2 tablespoons tamari

2 tablespoons apple cider vinegar

1 tablespoon + 1 teaspoon Dijon mustard

1 tablespoon balsamic vinegar

1 teaspoon dehydrated minced onion

1 teaspoon smoked paprika

¾ teaspoon garlic powder

¼ teaspoon red pepper flakes or to your preference

2–3 grinds black pepper

½ cup water

Preparation

1. Preheat the oven to 425°F and line a baking sheet with parchment paper. Spread the red onion, Yukon Gold potato, sweet potato, bell pepper, and cauliflower out in a single layer on the sheet pan and bake for 25 minutes.

2. Meanwhile, make the BBQ sauce. Add all sauce ingredients to a small pot and bring to a simmer. Stir and simmer for 2 to 3 minutes. Transfer the mix to a high-speed blender and blend on high until completely smooth. You can also do this in a food processor. Add water, 1 tablespoon at a time, if needed to assist blending. Set aside.

3. After 25 minutes, remove the veggies from the oven and transfer them to a bowl with the chickpeas and all the BBQ sauce. Mix well until everything is coated in sauce. Discard the parchment paper and put a new piece on the sheet pan if it's wet. Return the veggies and chickpeas to the pan and bake again for another 10 to 20 minutes until the veggies are tender and their edges are browned. Remove from the oven and serve immediately.

Variations: Use black beans instead of chickpeas.

Recipe Recycle: The BBQ sauce also pairs perfectly with B's Burger (page 189) or the fresh falafel from the Fresh Falafel & Tzatziki Bowl (page 171).

*If you have tough, dry dates, soak them for 15 to 30 minutes prior to making the sauce.

Sweet & Sour Chickpea-Stuffed Sweet Potatoes

These baked sweet potatoes are lick-your-plate delicious! Stuffed with chickpeas, broccoli, greens, and a sweet-and-sour sauce, they're a complete and satisfying meal.

Makes 4 servings

Ingredients

4 medium sweet potatoes

2 garlic cloves, minced

1 teaspoon finely grated ginger

¼ cup low-sodium tamari

¼ cup brown rice vinegar

3 tablespoons tomato paste

2 teaspoons vinegar-based hot sauce

2 tablespoons coconut sugar

1 cup red onion, diced

3 cups cooked or canned chickpeas, drained and rinsed

2 teaspoons arrowroot starch

½ cup water

4 cups bite-sized broccoli florets (1 large head broccoli)

1 cup finely chopped kale, spinach, or Swiss chard

Tahini Dill Sauce (optional)

¼ cup well-stirred tahini

3 tablespoons freshly squeezed lemon juice

1 garlic clove, minced

1½ teaspoons dried dill

1 teaspoon tamari

Garnishes

Fresh parsley, sesame seeds

Preparation

1. Preheat the oven to 450°F and line a baking sheet with parchment paper.

2. Scrub the sweet potatoes under running water and pierce each a few times with a paring knife. Bake the sweet potatoes for 45 to 60 minutes or until they're easily pierced with a fork and cooked throughout.

3. Meanwhile, make the Tahini Dill Sauce. Whisk all the sauce ingredients together in a small bowl. Add water, 1 tablespoon at a time, and mix again to reach a pourable consistency. Set aside.

4. Once the sweet potatoes are cooked, remove them from the oven and let them cool while you make the sweet-and-sour filling.

5. To make the sweet-and-sour filling, in a medium-sized bowl mix together the garlic, ginger, tamari, rice vinegar, tomato paste, hot sauce, and coconut sugar.

6. In a large sauté pan, sauté the red onion with a few tablespoons of water for 5 to 7 minutes or until the onion is translucent. Add the chickpeas and garlic/tamari mix and bring to a simmer. In a small bowl, mix the arrowroot starch with ½ cup of water and whisk together until dissolved. Add this to the pan and simmer over low heat for a

(Continued on next page)

Variations: Herbed Sunflower Dressing (page 119) and Tzatziki (page 171) are also wonderful alternatives to Tahini Dill Sauce. The sweet-and-sour filling is also delicious served over warm grains.

few minutes, uncovered, until the mixture begins to thicken.

7. Now, add the broccoli florets, cover, and continue to cook for another few minutes until the broccoli is bright green and tender. Finally, stir in the chopped kale, spinach, or Swiss chard and turn the heat off.

8. The sweet potatoes should be cool enough to handle now. Cut each potato in half and fluff the insides with a fork. Spoon the sweet-and-sour chickpea mix over the potato halves, drizzle with Tahini Dill Sauce, and garnish with parsley and sesame seeds.

The Blackout Burger

These tasty burgers are made with black rice and black beans as well as red onion and red beets. These rich and colorful foods make this burger an antioxidant powerhouse!

Makes 7 burgers

Ingredients

1 cup diced red onion

5 garlic cloves, minced

1 cup walnuts

1 cup roughly chopped raw red beets

1 cup cooked black rice (cooled to room temperature)

1½ cups cooked or canned black beans, drained and rinsed

½ cup gluten-free old-fashioned rolled oats

2 tablespoons brown rice flour

1 tablespoon + 1 teaspoon balsamic vinegar

2½ teaspoons ground coriander

1½ teaspoons ground cumin

1 teaspoon smoked paprika

¼ teaspoon red pepper flakes (more if you like it spicy)

¾ teaspoon sea salt

Preparation

1. Position the oven rack to the middle of the oven and preheat to 375°F. Line a baking sheet with parchment paper.

2. In a small sauté pan, sauté the onion with a few tablespoons of water for 5 to 7 minutes or until soft and translucent. Add the garlic and sauté for another minute, adding water as needed to prevent burning. Set aside.

3. Add the walnuts to a food processor and process until crumbly. Be careful not to overprocess the walnuts into a paste. Transfer the walnuts to a large bowl.

4. Next, add the chopped beets to the processor and process until finely chopped and roughly the same size as the crumbly walnuts. Transfer the beets to the bowl with the walnuts.

5. Now, add the cooked black rice, black beans, oats, brown rice flour, balsamic vinegar, coriander, cumin, smoked paprika, red pepper flakes, salt, and the cooked onion/garlic to the food processor. Process until the mix is well combined and most of the black beans are broken up.

6. Transfer the processed bean mix to the bowl with the walnuts and beets and mix well using a spatula.

7. The mix should be really thick. If you started with warm rice and the burger mix is still

(Continued on page 187)

Variation: If you don't have black rice, you can use brown.

warm, place the bowl in the fridge for 30 minutes to firm up. Otherwise, scoop out a little less than ½ cup of the mix and shape into a burger ¾-inch thick. Repeat with remaining mix, you should get 7 burgers.

8. Bake the burgers for 40 minutes then gently flip and bake for another 15 minutes. They're done when they're firm to the touch. Remove from the oven and let the burgers sit for 10 to 15 minutes. They'll firm as they cool. Serve the burgers on whole-grain buns or lettuce leaves. I like to top these with Tahini Dill Sauce (page 183) or Tzatziki (page 171).

B's Burger
(the *Best* Burger)

B (Bernard, my husband and full-time taste tester) would eat a burger for every meal if possible and this is his favorite (and mine too!). This burger is big and hearty and has flavors that work well however you top it. His favorite is with a smear of Sunflower Mozzarella (page 157), pickles, hot sauce, and crunchy lettuce. Mine is on lettuce leaves with BBQ sauce and red onion.

Makes 8–9 burgers

Ingredients

1 cup diced yellow onion

10 ounces button or cremini mushrooms, roughly chopped

1 cup roughly chopped red bell pepper

3 cups cooked or canned chickpeas, drained and rinsed

1 cup gluten-free old-fashioned rolled oats

½ cup pumpkin seeds

¼ cup ground flax seeds

3 tablespoons nutritional yeast

1 tablespoon coconut sugar

1 tablespoon white miso

3 tablespoons tamari

1 tablespoon apple cider or red wine vinegar

1 tablespoon dried oregano

1 tablespoon dried thyme

2½ teaspoons chili powder

1½ teaspoons garlic powder

½ teaspoon red pepper flakes

Heaping ¼ teaspoon ground allspice

Sea salt to taste

Preparation

1. Position the oven rack to the middle of the oven and preheat to 375°F. Line a baking sheet with parchment paper.

2. In a large sauté pan, sauté the onions with a few tablespoons of water until soft and translucent, about 5 to 7 minutes. Add water as needed to prevent burning. Now, add the mushrooms and bell pepper and continue to sauté for another 7 to 10 minutes, stirring often, until the mushrooms are browned and have shrunken and most of the liquid has evaporated. Drain any excess water from the pan—it's important that the veggies aren't wet—and set aside.

3. Add all remaining ingredients to a food processor along with the cooked onion, mushroom, and bell pepper. Process for 10 seconds, stop and scrape down the sides, and then process again until most of the chickpeas, oats, and pumpkin seeds are no longer whole. Taste the burger mix and reseason with salt if needed. Pulse again to combine. The burger dough will be thick.

4. Scoop out about ½ cup of the mix and shape into a burger ¾-inch to 1-inch thick and place on the baking sheet. Repeat with remaining burger dough.

(Continued on next page)

5. Bake the burgers for 40 minutes then gently flip and bake for another 15 minutes. The burgers are done when browned and firm to the touch. Remove the burgers from the oven and let them sit for 10 to 15 minutes. They'll firm as they cool.

6. You can enjoy these with all the burger fixings—whole-grain bread, ketchup, mustard, pickles. Or—and this is different but delicious—I often serve them with BBQ Sauce (page 180) and thinly sliced apple in a lettuce wrap.

Creamy Romesco & Roasted Cauliflower Penne

Romesco is a bold, smoky, tangy sauce originating from Spain. I like to make mine with whole almonds and home-roasted red peppers (how-to on the following page) or roasted red peppers packed in water. Paired with simple roasted cauliflower and whole grain or legume-based pasta, you have an easy yet elegant meal. If you like a really saucy pasta, double the sauce! Serve this on its own or with a simple side salad.

Makes 4 servings

Ingredients

6 cups bite-sized cauliflower florets (1 medium-
    large head cauliflower)
½ lemon
Sea salt and black pepper
12 ounces brown rice or red lentil penne

Romesco Sauce
⅓ cup whole almonds, soaked in water for
    6–8 hours
½ packed cup roasted red peppers (see how-to on
    page 193)
2 small garlic cloves
2 tablespoons tomato paste
1 tablespoon red wine vinegar
¾ teaspoon smoked paprika
⅛ teaspoon cayenne pepper
¼ teaspoon sea salt
½ cup water

Garnishes
¼ cup Hickory Almond Parmesan (page 149) or
    Bacon-ish Bits (page 116)

Preparation

1. Preheat the oven to 425°F and line a baking sheet with parchment paper.

2. Spread the cauliflower out on the pan, squeeze the lemon over the cauliflower, place the lemon on the sheet pan, and season the cauliflower with salt and several grinds of black pepper. Bake in the oven for 30 to 35 minutes, flipping halfway through, or until the cauliflower is tender and the edges of the florets begin to brown.

3. Meanwhile, make the Romesco sauce. Drain the almonds and discard the soaking water. Transfer the drained almonds and all other sauce ingredients to a high-speed blender and blend on high until completely smooth. Taste and reseason and add more water, 1 tablespoon at a time, and blend again if a thinner sauce is desired. Set aside.

4. Halfway through the cauliflower cooking time, bring a large pot of salted water to a boil and cook the pasta according to package directions for al dente. When the pasta is done, drain and return to the pot. You can serve this dish by dividing the pasta among bowls and then adding Romesco

(Continued on page 193)

Roasting Peppers

Whenever I use roasted red peppers, I roast my own—the bottled versions don't even compare! You can do this by preheating the oven to 450°F and placing whole peppers on a parchment-lined baking sheet. Bake in the oven for 45 minutes, flipping halfway through, or until the skins of the peppers are charred and wrinkled. Remove the peppers from the oven and place in a large bowl and cover the bowl with a large plate to trap the steam. Let sit for 15 minutes. This allows the peppers to sweat and makes removing their skins easier. When cool enough to handle, peel the skins off with your hands and remove the stems and seeds of each pepper and they're ready to use.

sauce or you can add all the Romesco sauce to the pasta and mix well. Once the pasta is plated, top with roasted cauliflower, another squeeze of the roasted lemon, and garnish with Hickory Almond Parmesan or Bacon-ish Bits.

Red Lentil Marinara Spaghetti

Hands down my favorite meal—saucy spaghetti! This is a recipe you can easily put into your weeknight rotation. Red lentils cook quickly and work to thicken and give texture to this vibrant marinara. You can serve this pasta topped with any Parmesan for extra yum!

Makes 4–6 servings

Ingredients

1 medium yellow onion, finely diced

2 medium carrots, finely diced

6 cloves garlic, minced

4 ounces button or cremini mushrooms, thinly sliced

1 teaspoon dried basil

¾ teaspoon dried thyme

½ teaspoon dried oregano

¼ teaspoon red pepper flakes or to your preference

1 (15 ounce) can tomato sauce

1 (14.5 ounce) can diced tomatoes (Italian-style or regular)

2 tablespoons tomato paste

2½ cups low-sodium vegetable broth

1 cup red lentils, rinsed

1 tablespoon balsamic vinegar

2 teaspoons coconut sugar, optional

½ teaspoon sea salt or to taste

2 cups baby spinach or 1 cup shredded kale

12–16 ounces brown rice or quinoa spaghetti

Parmesan of choice (page 149)

Preparation

1. In a large sauté pan, sauté the onion and carrots with about ¼ cup water for 5 to 7 minutes or until the onion is translucent. Add water as needed to prevent burning.

2. Now, add the garlic, mushrooms, basil, thyme, oregano, and red pepper flakes. Stir and continue to cook on medium heat for another 5 minutes. Again, add water as needed.

3. Add the tomato sauce, diced tomatoes, tomato paste, vegetable broth, and red lentils and stir. Cover the pan and bring to a simmer. Simmer for 10 minutes.

4. After 10 minutes, stir the marinara, partially remove the cover, and continue to simmer for another 10 to 12 minutes, stirring a couple of times throughout.

5. Most of the liquid in the marinara should be absorbed by now. Remove the cover and add the balsamic vinegar, coconut sugar, salt, baby spinach or kale, and cook for another minute. The greens will wilt quickly. Taste and reseason if needed and remove from heat.

6. Meanwhile, bring a large pot of water to boil and cook the pasta according to package directions for al dente texture. I really like my pasta saucy, so I make 12 ounces of pasta.

7. Once cooked, rinse and drain the pasta well. To serve, divide the pasta among plates and top with marinara. Garnish with Parmesan if desired.

Perfect Green-Pea Pesto Pasta

This is by far the best pesto-inspired recipe I've ever had! It's tangy and creamy and packed with phytonutrients. I like to mix in spinach with basil, but you can also use fresh kale. You'll be licking your plate!

Makes 4–6 servings

Ingredients

Pesto

2 cups frozen green peas

1½ packed cups fresh basil

1 packed cup baby spinach or kale

1 medium ripe avocado, pit removed and peeled

2 tablespoons nutritional yeast

2 tablespoons + 1 teaspoon freshly squeezed lemon juice

2 teaspoons white miso

2 garlic cloves, minced

¼ teaspoon red pepper flakes or to your preference

½ teaspoon sea salt or to taste

1 tablespoon water

Pasta

16 ounces brown rice or quinoa fusilli or farfalle

Classic Almond Parmesan (page 149)

Preparation

1. First, make the pesto. Thaw the green peas by putting them in a large bowl and covering them with boiling water for 2 to 3 minutes. The peas should turn a vibrant green. Drain the peas and add them along with all other pesto ingredients to a food processor. Process until no big pieces of basil, spinach/kale, or green peas are visible and the mixture is creamy. Stop and scrape down the processor a couple of times throughout. Add more water if needed, 1 tablespoon at a time, to achieve your desired consistency. Taste and reseason.

2. Cook the pasta according to package directions for al dente then rinse and drain well and return to the pot. Add half the pesto and toss with tongs until all the pasta is coated in pesto. Add as much pesto as you like. Divide among bowls and garnish with Parmesan. I like to serve this pasta with a side of roasted veggies or a light side salad. Keep any leftover pesto in a sealed container in the fridge for 2 to 3 days.

Variations: For a lighter option, use spiralized zucchini noodles instead of pasta and toss with sliced cherry tomatoes.

Market Shepherd's Pie

The first time I tried this recipe, I had just come from a fall farmers' market with a bag of root veggies. That might sound made up, but it's true! Shepherd's pie was a wholesome, sophisticated recipe that I'd never tackled, and I figured what better time! After many iterations, this is the version we love the most. I've added cauliflower to the top layer for extra cruciferous goodness. This is a big recipe with three parts—potato/cauliflower topping, lentil filling, and sauce. It's not complicated, but it requires more time than most other recipes. It is, however, well worth the work. I suggest preparing and chopping all the veg before starting so that it comes together smoothly.

Makes 6 servings

Ingredients

Potato/Cauliflower Layer

3 large Yukon Gold potatoes, peel on, roughly chopped

2 heaping cups bite-sized cauliflower florets

3 tablespoons nutritional yeast

1 teaspoon white miso

¼ cup unsweetened almond or organic soy milk (plus more if needed)

¼ teaspoon sea salt or to taste

Pie Filling

1 large yellow onion, diced

2 medium carrots, diced

2 stalks celery, thinly sliced

1 medium sweet potato, peel on, chopped into ½-inch cubes

4 garlic cloves, minced

2 teaspoons dried rosemary

1¾ teaspoons dried thyme

½ teaspoon dried parsley

½ teaspoon ground sage

¼ teaspoon red pepper flakes or to your preference

5 ounces button or cremini mushrooms, sliced

1½ cups cooked or canned brown lentils, drained and rinsed

2 teaspoons white wine vinegar

1 cup frozen green peas

Filling Sauce

1¾ cups low-sodium vegetable broth

3 tablespoons well-stirred tahini

1 tablespoon tamari

2 tablespoons white miso

2 teaspoons Dijon mustard

2 tablespoons arrowroot starch

2 tablespoons nutritional yeast

Garnishes

Nutritional yeast, sea salt, black pepper

(Continued on next page)

Preparation

1. First, make the potato layer. Add the chopped potatoes and cauliflower florets to a large pot of salted water. Bring to a boil and once boiling reduce to a simmer and simmer for 10 to 15 minutes or until the potatoes are very tender. Drain well and return to the pot. Add the nutritional yeast, miso, milk, and salt. Mash and add more milk as needed to get a creamy, but not wet, consistency. Set aside.

2. Meanwhile, make the pie filling. Preheat the oven to 400°F. In a large sauté pan, sauté the onion, carrots, celery, and sweet potato in about ¼ cup water for 10 minutes or until the onion is translucent and carrots soften. Stir occasionally and add more water as needed, 1 to 2 tablespoons at a time, to prevent burning.

3. Next, add the garlic, spices, and mushrooms and cover. Continue to cook on medium heat for another 5 minutes until the mushrooms release their juices and begin to brown. Remove the cover and stir a couple of times throughout. Add water if needed to prevent sticking.

4. Add the lentils and white wine vinegar and cook for another minute. Turn the heat off.

5. Then, make the filling sauce. Add all the sauce ingredients to a blender and blend until smooth.

6. Add the sauce to the pan of veggies and lentils and bring to a simmer. Simmer uncovered on low to medium heat for 5 minutes, stirring often, until the sauce thickens. Stir in the green peas and remove from heat.

7. Transfer the filling to a 13 x 9-inch (or similar) casserole dish. Be sure to get all the sauce out of the pan. Now, gently spread the potato layer over the filling by dropping spoonful along the top and spreading it together with the back of a spoon or spatula. Sprinkle extra nutritional yeast, salt, and a few grinds of black pepper over the top.

8. Place the casserole dish in the preheated oven and lay a sheet pan underneath the casserole dish in case the filling bubbles over. Bake the shepherd's pie for 30 minutes uncovered. The potato layer should firm up and brown in the corners and you might be able to see the sauce bubbling in the corners. Remove from the oven and let rest for at least 15 minutes before serving.

Variation: Use 2 additional potatoes instead of cauliflower for the top layer if desired.

Vegetable Lasagna & Tofu Ricotta with House Marinara

A layered, saucy, creamy lasagna sans cheese! This recipe was created for a cooking class I taught called Soy Confused, a workshop focused on understanding different soy products and how to use them. This indulgent lasagna is a great example of the versatility of tofu, like in making "ricotta!" It's a great veggie-driven, family meal that everyone will love. If using House Marinara (page 204), make ahead of time to shorten prep work.

Makes 9–12 servings

Ingredients

Tofu Ricotta

1 (12–14 oz package) extra-firm organic tofu, pressed (see page 17 for how-to)
¼ cup white miso
¼ cup well-stirred tahini
2 tablespoons nutritional yeast
1½ teaspoons garlic powder
1 teaspoon dried basil
1 teaspoon dried oregano
1 teaspoon onion powder
¼ teaspoon sea salt
3 tablespoons freshly squeezed lemon juice
Scant ½ cup water

Vegetables

1 medium red onion, finely diced
3 medium carrots, finely diced
8 ounces button mushrooms, thinly sliced
1 head broccoli, finely chopped (4 cups)
2 cups packed baby spinach

Assembly

6 cups vegan marinara sauce (or 2 batches House Marinara, page 204)
12 ounces oven-ready, brown rice lasagna noodles*
½ cup any Parmesan (page 149), optional
Fresh basil, optional

Preparation

1. Preheat the oven to 375°F. Break the tofu into chunks and place in a food processor or high-speed blender. Add all other ricotta ingredients in the order listed and process/blend continuously until smooth, scraping down the sides of the processor/blender a couple of times throughout. Set aside.

2. In a large nonstick sauté pan, sauté the onion and carrots with a few tablespoons of water for 10 minutes. Add water as needed to prevent burning. Now, add the mushrooms and broccoli and sauté for another 5 minutes, stirring often, until the mushrooms release their juices and the broccoli turns bright green and is just tender. Stir in the spinach and turn the heat off. Pour off any excess liquid.

3. Add the tofu ricotta to the pan and mix well using a spatula and set aside.

(Continued on page 203)

---

* When using oven-ready noodles, it's important to cover the noodles completely with sauce (especially the top layer). If using traditional lasagna noodles, cook the noodles in a large pot of boiling water 2 minutes short of al dente, transfer to a bowl of water to cool, pat dry, and follow the recipe as written.

4. Now, assemble the lasagna. Spread 1½ cups of marinara along the bottom of a 3-inch-deep, 13 x 9-inch casserole dish. Next, layer 3 to 4 lasagna noodles side by side with a little space between each noodle, being careful not to overlap the noodles (depending on the shape and size of the dish you're using, you may need to crack some noodles in half to fill in space). Then, evenly spread 2 heaping cups of the veggie ricotta mix over the noodles. This is one layer. Start the next layer with 1 cup of marinara, 3 more lasagna noodles, 2 cups veggie ricotta mix, and so on. You should get 3 layers and then finish with a final layer of noodles and 1½ cups marinara. Spread Parmesan on top if desired.

5. Cover the lasagna with tinfoil and bake for 30 minutes. After 30 minutes, remove the tinfoil and bake uncovered for another 20 minutes or until the sauce is bubbling.

6. Remove from the oven and let the lasagna rest, covered, for at least 15 minutes before slicing into 9 to 12 pieces. Garnish with basil if desired.

House Marinara

This is a multipurpose marinara sauce. It's easy to make and freezes wonderfully. You can use this in any recipe where marinara is called for.

Makes 3 cups

Ingredients

Marinara
½ cup finely diced red onion
3 garlic cloves, minced
1½ teaspoons dried oregano
½ teaspoon dried basil
Pinch red pepper flakes
1 (28 ounce) can crushed tomatoes
2 tablespoons tomato paste
1 teaspoon coconut sugar, optional
2 teaspoons balsamic vinegar
¼ teaspoon sea salt or to taste

Preparation

1. In a medium-sized pot, sauté the onion with a few tablespoons of water for 5 to 7 minutes until the onions are translucent. Add the garlic, oregano, basil, and red pepper flakes and continue to simmer for another 2 minutes.

2. Add the crushed tomatoes and tomato paste and bring to a simmer. Partially cover and simmer for 30 to 35 minutes. Once the sauce has reduced and thickened, stir in the coconut sugar (if using), balsamic vinegar, and salt and simmer for another minute. Remove from heat and set aside until needed.

3. If you want a smooth sauce, transfer the marinara to a blender and blend until smooth. Once cooled, keep in the fridge for up to 5 days or freeze for up to 3 months.

One-Pot Broccoli Hummus Mac n' Cheeze

In the name of easy, nutrient-dense pasta you can make in less than thirty minutes, I give you my cheezy mac n'cheese! This recipe involves so many of my favorite things: pasta, hummus, one-pot meals. The cheezy sauce was inspired by hummus where chickpeas are blended into a creamy consistency. The Parmesan is optional but definitely adds a special touch.

Makes 4 servings

Ingredients

Cheezy Hummus Sauce

1 cup chopped yellow onion

4 garlic cloves, chopped

1½ cups cooked or canned chickpeas, drained and rinsed

2 tablespoons nutritional yeast

2 tablespoons freshly squeezed lemon juice

1 tablespoon tamari

1 tablespoon Dijon mustard

½ teaspoon ground turmeric

¼ teaspoon red pepper flakes or to your preference

½ cup unsweetened almond or organic soy milk (plus more if needed)

Pasta

12 ounces brown-rice elbow macaroni

5 heaping cups bite-sized broccoli florets (2 small heads broccoli)

1 cup frozen green peas

¼ cup Parmesan of choice (page 149), plus more as needed, optional

Preparation

1. First, make the Cheezy Hummus Sauce. Add the onion and garlic to a small sauté pan with a few tablespoons of water and sauté for 5 to 7 minutes until the onion is soft and translucent. Add water as needed to prevent burning.

2. Add the cooked onion/garlic mix to a blender along with all other sauce ingredients and blend until completely smooth. Add more milk, 1 tablespoon at a time, if needed to get a smooth, pourable, but thick sauce. Set aside.

3. Bring a large pot of salted water to a boil. Once boiling, add the pasta and cook according to package directions for al dente. When there's 3 minutes of cooking time remaining for the pasta, add the broccoli to the pot. When the cooking time is up, turn the heat off, and add the peas to the pot. Let everything sit for a minute until the peas are bright green, then drain pasta, broccoli, and peas well in a colander and return to the pot.

4. Add the cheezy hummus sauce and ¼ cup Parmesan (if using) and mix. Divide the pasta among bowls and garnish each with a sprinkle of additional Parmesan if desired.

Weeknight Tempeh & Vegetable Casserole

My years of recipe testing have turned me into a very culinarily curious person. I love mixing stuff together and just shoving it in the oven to see what happens! A lot of my kitchen sorcery fails, but not this time! What started as an experiment has become our favorite weeknight meal that's also nutritionally balanced and veggie forward. The tempeh, veggies, and sauce which thickens in the oven (I know, ah-mazing!) are baked then served over rice. I like to rotate between broccoli and asparagus, depending on what's available.

Makes 4 servings

Ingredients

2 medium red or yellow onions, thinly sliced

4 heaping cups bite-sized broccoli florets or 1-inch pieces of asparagus

2 large carrots, sliced into ¼-inch rounds or half-moons

1 (8 ounce) package tempeh, diced into ¾-inch cubes

1¼ cups dry brown rice

Optional Garnish

3 scallions, thinly sliced

Sauce

¼ cup + 2 tablespoons low-sodium tamari

3 tablespoons well-stirred creamy almond butter

3 tablespoons freshly squeezed orange juice

2 tablespoons rice wine vinegar

3 garlic cloves, chopped

2½ teaspoons finely grated ginger

1 tablespoon arrowroot starch

1½ teaspoon vinegar-based hot sauce

⅓ cup water

1 teaspoon coconut sugar, optional

Preparation

1. Preheat the oven to 425°F. Mix the onion, broccoli or asparagus, carrots, and tempeh together in a 9 x 13-inch, or similar, casserole dish. Set aside.

2. Make the sauce by adding all the sauce ingredients to a blender. Blend until completely smooth. The sauce will be thin.

3. Pour the sauce over the veggies and tempeh and mix. Cover the casserole dish tightly with tinfoil and bake for 45 to 55 minutes or until the sauce is bubbling and the veggies are tender. Stir the veggies and tempeh 1 to 2 times throughout for even cooking.

4. Meanwhile, cook the brown rice according to package directions. Once cooked, fluff with a fork, cover, and set aside until the casserole is done.

5. Serve the tempeh, veggies, and sauce on top of brown rice and garnish with scallions.

Variations: Use tahini instead of almond butter to make it nut-free.

SWEETS & TREATS

DESSERT MAKEOVER

I have a sweet tooth and it took me a long time to cut back on sweets, even the healthier kind. If you're currently making the transition to a more whole-foods diet, you might still have strong sugar cravings. But, over time and as you reduce the amount of sugar in your diet, you'll notice that you become more sensitive to sugar—especially processed varieties.

When I want a no-added-sugar treat, I generally opt for a Mint Chocolate-Caramel Chew (page 222), Lemon-Turmeric Bliss Balls (page 214) or an indulgent Raw Cinnamon Roll (page 237)—I love a little something I can eat right out of the freezer!

Other recipes in this chapter are ideal for special occasions and celebrations (with a couple of seasonal favorites as well) and all leftovers can be frozen for later.

Easy Apple-Berry Crumble   213

Lemon-Turmeric Bliss Balls   214

Pumpkin Pie Squares   217

Country Date Squares   219

Mint Chocolate-Caramel Chews   222

Gingerbread Cloud Cookies   225

Mango Truffles   226

Black-Velvet Chocolate Cake   229

New York–Style Baked Chocolate-Swirl Cheesecake   231

Carrot Cake & Citrus Cream-Cheese Icing   235

Raw Cinnamon Rolls   237

Chocolate Lover Brownies   241

Easy Apple-Berry Crumble

This is a light, fruit-centric dessert that can also double as breakfast! I like to serve it with Almond Butter Caramel but it's also delicious on its own or with banana "nice" cream.

Makes 4–6 servings

Ingredients

1½ cup gluten-free old-fashioned rolled oats

1 tablespoon coconut sugar

1¼ teaspoons cinnamon

¼ teaspoon ground allspice

¼ teaspoon sea salt

3 tablespoons maple syrup

1 tablespoon well-stirred almond or sunflower seed butter

½ teaspoon pure vanilla extract

2 apples, peel left on, chopped in ½-inch cubes (2 heaping cups)

3 cups mixed frozen berries (blueberries, raspberries, and blackberries work well)

1 teaspoon arrowroot starch

Almond Butter Caramel (page 45), optional

Preparation

1. Position the oven rack in the middle of the oven and preheat the oven to 350°F.

2. Mix the oats, coconut sugar, cinnamon, allspice, and salt in a medium-sized bowl.

3. In a separate small bowl, whisk together the maple syrup, almond or sunflower seed butter, and vanilla. Pour this into the bowl of oats and mix together with a nonstick spatula until no dry spots remain. Set aside.

4. In a 6- to 8-inch-square baking dish (no need to line with parchment paper) mix together the apples and berries. Sprinkle the arrowroot starch over the fruit and mix.

5. Using your hands, spread the oat mixture on top of the fruit.

6. Cover the baking dish with tinfoil and bake in the oven for 20 minutes. Then, remove the tinfoil and continue baking for another 40 minutes or until the top is browned and the berries are bubbling in the corners of the dish.

7. Remove from the oven and let the crumble rest for 10 minutes. Drizzle with Almond Butter Caramel, if desired, and serve.

Lemon-Turmeric Bliss Balls

Perfect for snacks or a light dessert, these bliss balls have no added sugar and are rich in anti-inflammatory compounds. The lemon zest and juice combine to make these bliss balls bright and slightly tart.

Makes 12 balls

Ingredients

1¼ cups gluten-free old-fashioned rolled oats

1 packed cup pitted, soft Medjool dates

2 tablespoons chia seeds

2 tablespoons hemp seeds

Zest of 1 lemon

3 tablespoons freshly squeezed lemon juice

¾ teaspoon ground turmeric

¼ teaspoon cinnamon

1 teaspoon pure vanilla extract

Rolling Garnish

⅓ cup unsweetened coconut, hemp, or sesame seeds

Preparation

1. Place all ingredients, except for rolling garnish, in a food processor and process until the mixture is well combined and the dates are broken up. The mix should stick together when you squeeze it between your fingers. Add water, a couple of teaspoons at a time, and process again to combine if the mix isn't sticking together.

2. Scoop out about 2 tablespoons of the mixture (I like to use a ¾-ounce spring-release scoop or disher, see page 11) and shape into a tight ball. Roll in coconut, hemp, or sesame seeds. Keep in the fridge in a sealed container for up to 5 days or keep in the freezer for up to 3 months.

Pumpkin Pie Squares

These squares have a lightly sweetened crust and a creamy, pumpkin-almond butter filling that will hit that sweet spot! Remember to let the squares cool and set before cutting.

Makes 16 squares

Ingredients

Crust

1 cup gluten-free oat flour

¾ cup blanched almond flour

¼ cup coconut sugar

¼ teaspoon sea salt

½ cup unsweetened applesauce

¼ teaspoon almond extract

Pumpkin Layer

⅓ packed cup pitted Medjool or Deglet Nour
   dates, soaked in hot water for 15–30 minutes

1⅓ cup unsweetened pumpkin puree

¼ cup well-stirred almond butter

2 teaspoons pure vanilla extract

¼ cup coconut sugar

1 tablespoon arrowroot starch

1 teaspoon blackstrap or regular molasses

1 teaspoon pumpkin pie spice

½ teaspoon cinnamon

Pinch sea salt

1 tablespoon unsweetened almond milk, if needed

Preparation

1. Position the oven rack in the middle of the oven and preheat to 350°F. Line an 8 x 8-inch square baking pan with parchment paper so that the parchment paper hangs out over opposing sides.

2. First, make the crust. Place the oat flour, almond flour, coconut sugar, and salt in a medium bowl and mix. Then, add the applesauce and almond extract and, with slightly damp hands, knead the crust together until no dry spots remain. Press the crust evenly into the parchment-paper-lined baking pan, being sure to work it into the corners and smooth out the surface so it's even. Bake the crust for 10 minutes, then remove from the oven and set aside.

3. Now, make the pumpkin layer. Drain the dates, discard the soaking water, and add the drained dates and all other filling ingredients (except almond milk) to a high-speed blender. With the assistance of the blender's tamper, blend the mixture on high until completely smooth. Add 1 tablespoon of almond milk if needed to assist the blending.

4. Spread the pumpkin mixture evenly onto the baked crust using a nonstick spatula. Return the pan to the oven and bake for 35 minutes. The top will be browned and firm to the touch when done.

(Continued on next page)

5. Remove the squares from the oven and let cool completely in the pan on a cooling rack, then transfer the pan to the fridge for 3 hours to allow the filling to set. When the pumpkin is set, remove the squares from the pan by pulling on the parchment paper and place onto a cutting board. Use a sharp knife (not serrated) and cut into 16 squares. Keep the squares in the fridge for up to 5 days or keep in the freezer for up to 3 months.

Country Date Squares

This is a classic and essential dessert recipe where I come from (beautiful Newfoundland), but with a nutritional makeover. The recipe has two parts; the crust (used for the top and bottom) and the filling. Both the crust and the filling require soaked dates and it's best to measure and soak them separately.

Makes 12–16 squares

Ingredients

Crust

1½ teaspoons whole psyllium husk

¼ cup water

1 cup gluten-free oat flour

1½ cup gluten-free old-fashioned rolled oats, divided

⅓ cup blanched almond flour

2 tablespoons ground flax seeds

½ teaspoon baking soda

¼ teaspoon cinnamon

½ teaspoon sea salt

½ packed cup pitted Medjool dates, soaked.in hot water for 15–30 minutes

¾ cup whole walnuts

⅓ cup unsweetened applesauce

2 tablespoons maple syrup

1 teaspoon orange zest

2 tablespoon freshly squeezed orange juice

1 teaspoon pure vanilla extract

Filling

1½ packed cups pitted Medjool dates, soaked in hot water for 15–30 minutes

½ cup dried cranberries

¼ cup water

½ teaspoon sea salt

Preparation

1. Soak the dates for the crust and filling in hot water and in separate bowls. Position the oven rack in the middle of the oven and preheat to 350°F. Line an 8 x 8-inch square baking pan with parchment paper so that the parchment paper is hanging out over opposing sides.

2. First make the crust. In a small bowl, mix the psyllium husk with ¼ cup of water and set aside for 5 minutes to thicken. Add the oat flour, rolled oats, almond flour, flax seeds, baking soda, cinnamon, and salt to a large bowl and mix together. Set aside.

3. Now, drain the crust's dates (½ cup) well, discard the soaking liquid, and place the drained dates in a food processor with the walnuts. Pulse 7 to 10 times to break them up. Add the applesauce, maple syrup, orange zest and juice, vanilla, and thickened psyllium/water mix to the processor along with dates/walnuts and process until a thick paste is reached. Stop and scrape down the sides 2 to 3 times throughout.

4. Remove this mix from the food processor and transfer to the bowl of dry crust ingredients. Mix together with a nonstick spatula or knead with damp hands until no dry spots remain. The mix will be thick. Set aside.

(Continued on page 221)

5. Now, make the filling. Drain the filling dates (1½ cups) well, lightly squeezing out and discarding the soaking water, and add the drained dates, cranberries, water, and salt to the food processor and process until a rough paste has formed. Stop and scrape down the sides of the processor as often as needed. You want the filling to be thick and almost smooth.

6. With damp hands, spread half the crust dough along the bottom of the parchment-lined pan. Do this by dropping the dough along the bottom of the pan, pressing it together, and shaping it into the pan.

7. Now, spread the filling evenly over the crust using a nonstick spatula. Finally, spread the remaining crust dough on top of the filling by dropping spoonsful randomly over the top and lightly pushing them into each other. The top should have a bumpy, rustic texture.

8. Bake the date squares for 18 to 20 minutes. The top will be slightly firm to the touch.

9. Transfer the pan to a cooling rack and let the date squares cool completely in the pan. Once completely cooled, lift the date squares out of the pan by pulling on the parchment paper. Use a sharp chef's knife (not a serrated knife) to cut into 12 to 16 squares.

Mint Chocolate-Caramel Chews

These caramels were inspired by after-dinner mints. Unlike traditional caramels made with uber-processed ingredients and lots of sugar, these caramels are made with brain-healthy walnuts and creamy Medjool dates. They're minty, chewy, and mildly addictive. My favorite way to eat these delicious chews is right out of the freezer.

Makes 25 chews

Ingredients

½ cup walnuts, soaked in warm water for 2–3 hours

½ packed cup pitted, soft Medjool dates

¼ cup + 1 tablespoon unsweetened cocoa or cacao powder

½ teaspoon pure peppermint extract

¼ teaspoon sea salt

Preparation

1. Drain the walnuts, discard the soaking liquid, and place the drained walnuts in a food processor with the pitted dates, cocoa or cacao powder, mint extract, and salt.

2. Process continuously. The mix will first turn into crumbles but will eventually stick together and start rolling around in a ball. Scrape down the container a couple of times throughout. The dough should be smooth with no chunks of nuts. This may take a few minutes. Add 1 to 2 teaspoons water to help the mix stick together if it's not coming together.

3. Transfer the "dough" onto a piece of parchment paper and shape into a rough square. Cover with another piece of parchment paper and use a rolling pin to shape the dough into a 4-inch square that's about ¾-inch thick. You can also do this with your hands. I like to dampen a chef's knife and press the side of the blade against the edges of the square to create straight, clean edges.

4. Place the dough in the freezer for one hour to set. Remove from the freezer and use a sharp knife to cut the dough into 25 caramels, wiping the knife clean between each cut. Separate the caramels and place them on a plate or in a container in a single layer and keep them in the fridge, uncovered, for 12 to 24 hours. They'll dry out and firm up. Keep in a sealed container in the fridge for up to a week or keep them in the freezer for 3 months.

Gingerbread Cloud Cookies

A holiday staple, these cookies are soft, almost fluffy, with deep gingerbread flavor. The combination of bitter blackstrap molasses, caramel-y coconut sugar, and ginger make for a rich and festive cookie. I suggest using a spring-release scoop or disher to shape the cookies.

Makes 14–16 cookies

Ingredients

Dry

⅔ cup brown rice flour

⅔ cup blanched almond flour

⅓ cup coconut sugar

2 tablespoons arrowroot starch

1¼ teaspoons ground ginger

1 teaspoon cinnamon

¾ teaspoon pumpkin pie spice

1 teaspoon baking powder

½ teaspoon baking soda

¼ teaspoon sea salt

Wet

3 tablespoons blackstrap molasses

2 tablespoons freshly squeezed orange juice

¼ cup unsweetened almond milk or organic soy milk

1 teaspoon pure vanilla extract

Variations: You can use regular molasses instead of blackstrap.

Preparation

1. Position the oven rack in the middle of the oven and preheat to 350°F. Line a baking sheet with parchment paper and set aside.

2. In a large bowl, mix all the dry ingredients, breaking up any clumps of almond flour or coconut sugar.

3. In a separate small bowl, whisk together the wet ingredients.

4. Add the wet ingredients to the dry and combine using a spatula until all the ingredients are incorporated. The dough will seem wet; this is normal.

5. Use a ¾-ounce spring-release scoop or disher to scoop out the dough and transfer to the sheet pan. Leave at least 1 inch between each cookie as they'll spread. If you don't have a disher, scoop out a heaping tablespoon of dough for each cookie and shape into a ball with damp hands. The cookies might not be perfect circles, but they'll still taste great.

6. Now, use a wet fork (this helps prevent sticking) and gently press down the center of each cookie so they're 2 inches in diameter. I like to keep a glass of water nearby and dip the fork in water between pressing each cookie.

7. Bake for 14 to 16 minutes until they're slightly firm to the touch but give a little when pressed. Remove from the oven and let cool completely on the pan. They'll firm up as they cool but are intended to be soft and chewy. Keep in the fridge for 2 to 3 days or freeze for up to 3 months.

Mango Truffles

There is something extra special about these fruit and nut balls, and I felt they deserved a categorical upgrade to "truffles." They're sweet and fresh, simple and sophisticated. Dried mango adds a tropical and unexpected delicious twist! I like to use white chia seeds in this recipe simply for the color, but you can use black chia seeds if that's what you have on hand.

Makes 12–13 truffles

Ingredients

1 cup whole cashews

1 packed cup dried mango, roughly chopped

¾ cup gluten-free old-fashioned rolled oats

2 tablespoons white chia seeds

1 tablespoon well-stirred tahini

1 tablespoon maple syrup

¼ teaspoon pure vanilla extract

¼ teaspoon cinnamon

¼ teaspoon sea salt

1–2 tablespoons almond milk, if needed

Rolling Garnish

⅓ cup unsweetened coconut or hemp seeds

Preparation

1. Add all the ingredients, except rolling garnishes, to a food processor and process continuously until the mixture reaches a fine, crumbly texture. The mixture should stick together when pressed firmly between your fingers. If the mix is too crumbly to stick together, add 1 tablespoon of milk and process again.

2. Scoop out about 2 tablespoon of the mix (I like to use a ¾-ounce spring-release scoop or disher) and roll into a ball, pressing firmly between your hands. Roll in optional coconut or hemp seeds. Repeat with remaining mixture. Keep in the fridge for up to 3 days or in the freezer for up to 3 months.

Black-Velvet Chocolate Cake

I'm bringing Bundt cakes back! They're beautiful, and the shape of a Bundt pan almost guarantees easy, even baking. I prefer a silicone pan to prevent sticking. This is my staple chocolate cake with an icing made from black beans and hemp seeds—your guests get a hit of protein, fiber, essential minerals, and anti-inflammatory fats with their dessert! Be sure to let the cake cool completely before icing.

Makes 12–16 slices

Ingredients

Cake

2 tablespoons whole psyllium husk

1 cup water

2½ cups blanched almond flour

1½ cups coconut sugar

2½ cups gluten-free oat flour

1½ cups unsweetened cocoa powder

2 tablespoons baking powder

2 teaspoons baking soda

¾ teaspoon sea salt

1½ cups unsweetened almond milk or organic soy milk

½ cup unsweetened applesauce

½ cup maple syrup

Black Velvet Icing

¾ packed cup pitted Medjool or Deglet Nour dates, soaked in hot water for 15–30 minutes

1½ cups cooked or canned black beans, drained and rinsed

¼ cup unsweetened cocoa powder

¼ cup maple syrup

2 tablespoons hemp seeds

1 teaspoon pure vanilla extract

¼ cup unsweetened almond milk or organic soy milk (plus more if needed)

Pinch sea salt

Optional Garnish

4 cups fresh berries

Preparation

1. Position the oven rack in the middle of the oven and preheat to 350°F.

2. Add the psyllium husk to a small bowl with 1 cup of water. Mix and set aside for 5 minutes to thicken.

3. Add the almond flour and coconut sugar to large bowl and mix together, breaking up any clumps with your hands or the back of a spoon. Now, add the oat flour, cocoa powder, baking powder, baking soda, and salt to the bowl and mix together until well combined. Set aside.

4. Add the psyllium husk mix, almond or soy milk, applesauce, and maple syrup to a blender and blend until combined.

5. Add the blended wet ingredients to the dry ingredients and mix well until no dry spots remain.

6. Transfer the batter to a nonstick Bundt pan. Place the Bundt pan directly on the oven rack and bake for 50 to 60 minutes. The cake is done when it's firm to the touch and has pulled away from the sides of the pan.

7. While the cake is baking, make the icing. Drain the dates, discard the soaking water, and add the drained dates and all other icing

(Continued on next page)

ingredients to a high-speed blender. Blend on high until completely smooth. If your blender has a tamper, use this to assist the blending. The texture should be thick and smooth. Add more milk, 1 tablespoon at a time, to thin the icing if desired. Transfer to a bowl, cover, and place in fridge to set.

8. When the cake is done, remove it from the oven and let it cool for 20 minutes in the Bundt pan on a cooling rack. Then, invert the cake onto the cooling rack and gently remove from the pan (it should pop out easily). Let the cake cool completely. Once cooled, transfer to a serving tray and cover in icing. Serve as is or decorate the cake with fresh berries for a burst of color. Use a sharp chef's knife to slice the cake.

New York–Style Baked Chocolate-Swirl Cheesecake

A lot of vegan cheesecakes are a) made almost entirely from coconut oil or b) like ice cream cakes where they're kept in and served from the freezer, and I love those! But I tried for almost a year to make a creamy yet firm baked plant-based cheesecake that could be served at room temperature without the risk of melting. And I finally nailed it! I like to make this when I'm serving a crowd and need a dessert I can make ahead of time that has that wow factor.

Makes 12–16 servings

Ingredients

Crust

2 teaspoons whole psyllium husk

¼ cup water

2 cups gluten-free old-fashioned rolled oats

1 cup sunflower seeds

3 tablespoons unsweetened cocoa powder

3 tablespoons coconut sugar

½ teaspoon cinnamon

½ teaspoon sea salt

¼ cup maple syrup

Filling

2 cups cashews, soaked in water for 4 hours

½ cup maple syrup

1 (12 ounce) block extra-firm silken tofu, drained

3 tablespoons arrowroot starch

¼ cup coconut sugar

2 tablespoons freshly squeezed lemon juice

1 tablespoon pure vanilla extract

Pinch sea salt

Chocolate Swirl

2 tablespoons Filling

2 teaspoons unsweetened cocoa powder

1 teaspoon maple syrup

Preparation

1. Position the oven rack in the middle of the oven and preheat to 350°F. Line the bottom of an 8-inch springform pan with parchment paper. Do this by tracing the outline of the springform pan insert onto the parchment paper and cutting it out. Connect the base (with parchment paper) and outside ring of the springform pan.

2. First, make the crust. In a small bowl, mix the psyllium husk with ¼ cup water and set aside for 5 minutes to thicken.

3. Add the oats, sunflower seeds, cocoa powder, coconut sugar, cinnamon, salt, and thickened psyllium/water mix to a food processor. Pulse 5 to 6 times to combine, then process continuously. Pour the maple syrup through the feed tube as the crust ingredients process. The crust will begin to stick together. Add 1 or 2 teaspoons of water if the crust is too dry until it forms into a ball and rolls around the processor.

4. Remove the crust from the processor and transfer to the parchment-paper-lined springform pan. Press the crust into the pan,

(Continued on page 233)

Variations: Skip the chocolate swirl and make a "vanilla" version, or you can replace the cocoa powder with matcha powder and make a Matcha Swirl Cheesecake.

starting in the middle and working outward and halfway up the sides (about 1½ inches) of the pan. Set aside.

5. Now, make the filling. Drain the cashews, discard the soaking liquid, and add the drained cashews and all other filling ingredients to a high-speed blender. Blend the mix on high, using your tamper to assist, until completely smooth.

6. Remove 2 tablespoons of the filling and set aside in a small bowl. Pour the rest of the filling into the springform pan and smooth out the surface using a silicone spatula.

7. Now, make the chocolate swirl. In the small bowl with 2 tablespoons of filling, add 2 teaspoons cocoa powder and 1 teaspoon maple syrup. Whisk together until smooth. Drop small dollops of the mix randomly across the top of the cheesecake and then drag a butter knife through to create a swirl effect.

8. Place the cheesecake in the oven for 45 to 50 minutes until the top is golden in color and dry to the touch. Remove from the oven and place on a cooling rack and let cool completely. The filling might be slightly soft but shouldn't look wet. It will firm as it cools.

9. When cooled completely, run a thin spatula around the edge of the cake to loosen it from the pan (I like to use the long, thin spatulas that come from Vitamix). Release the springform pan ring.

10. Transfer the cake to a cutting board and use a sharp chef's knife to make 12 to 16 slices. To ensure clean, neat slices, wipe your knife with a damp dishcloth between slicing. Keep this cheesecake in the fridge in a sealed container for 3 to 5 days or freeze for up to 3 months.

Carrot Cake & Citrus Cream-Cheese Icing

This cake is ah-mazing! It's served as everything from birthday cake to holiday dessert and everyone always wants seconds. You need a high-speed blender to make the icing, but you can also skip the icing and serve the cake plain.

Makes 8–12 servings

Ingredients

1 tablespoon whole psyllium husk
½ cup water
1 loosely packed cup grated carrot
1½ cups gluten-free oat flour
1¼ cups blanched almond flour
¾ cup coconut sugar
½ cup raisins, optional
1 tablespoon baking powder
1 teaspoon baking soda
1½ teaspoons cinnamon
½ teaspoon ground ginger
¼ teaspoon ground cloves
¼ teaspoon ground allspice
¼ teaspoon ground nutmeg
½ teaspoon sea salt
¾ cup unsweetened almond milk
1 tablespoon pure vanilla extract

Citrus Cream-Cheese Icing
1 cup cashews, soaked in water for 2–3 hours
1 teaspoon orange zest
2 tablespoons freshly squeezed orange juice
¼ cup maple syrup
1 teaspoon pure vanilla extract
½ teaspoon cinnamon
⅛ teaspoon sea salt
1 tablespoon unsweetened almond milk

Optional Garnish
½ cup crushed walnuts or 1 cup blueberries

Preparation

1. Position the oven rack in the middle of the oven, preheat to 350°F, and line an 8-inch circular cake pan with parchment paper. Do this by tracing the bottom of the cake pan onto parchment paper and cutting it out.

2. Mix 1 tablespoon psyllium husk with ½ cup of water in a small bowl and set aside for 5 minutes to thicken.

3. Grate the carrot using the small-hole side of a box grater and set aside.

4. In a large bowl, mix the oat flour, almond flour, coconut sugar, raisins, baking powder, baking soda, all the spices, and salt, making sure all the clumps of almond flour and coconut sugar are broken up.

5. Next, add the almond milk, vanilla, and the psyllium/water mix to the bowl of dry ingredients and mix together until no clumps or dry spots remain. Stir in the grated carrot.

6. Pour the batter into the parchment-paper-lined pan and spread it evenly using a nonstick spatula.

7. Bake the cake for 40 to 45 minutes or until firm to the touch and the edges begin to pull away from the pan.

8. When the cake is done, remove it from the oven and let it cool completely in the pan

(Continued on next page)

on a cooling rack. When completely cooled, place a flat serving plate or cutting board on top of the cake pan and flip to release the cake, it should easily pop out. Gently peel the parchment paper off the cake.

9. While the cake is baking/cooling, make the icing. Drain the cashews, discard the soaking water, and add the drained cashews and all other icing ingredients, except almond milk, to a high-speed blender and blend until completely smooth. Add 1 tablespoon of almond milk if needed to get a smooth consistency. Refrigerate the icing until needed.

10. Spread half the icing on top of the cake using a spatula. I think this is the perfect cake-to-icing ratio, but you can add more if desired. Garnish the circumference of the cake with crushed nuts or fresh berries, if desired. Slice the cake using a sharp chef's knife, wiping the knife clean between slices. Leftovers (icing and all) can be frozen for up to 3 months.

Raw Cinnamon Rolls

Roll up your sleeves for these outstanding cinnamon rolls! This raw recipe (meaning no baking is required) has two parts; the dough and the filling. Both are made in a food processor. This recipe does require some soaking before and freezing after so it's best to make ahead of time and read carefully before starting in. I prefer raw almond butter in this recipe, but you can also use roasted.

Makes 16 cinnamon rolls

Ingredients

Dough

1 cup whole almonds

1 cup gluten-free old-fashioned rolled oats

¼ cup ground flax seeds

1½ packed cups pitted, soft Medjool dates

1 teaspoon cinnamon

1 teaspoon pure vanilla extract

Pinch sea salt

1 tablespoon water

Filling

¾ cup raisins + ¼ cup dried cranberries, soaked in the same bowl of warm water for 1 hour

¼ cup well-stirred almond butter

1 tablespoon cinnamon

¼ teaspoon sea salt

Preparation

1. To make the dough, add the almonds to a food processor and process for 10 to 15 seconds or until the almonds are mostly broken up.

2. Add the oats, flax seeds, pitted dates, cinnamon, vanilla, and salt and process continuously. Pour 1 tablespoon of water into the feeding tube and process until the mix sticks together and starts rolling around in a smooth ball; this will take 1 to 2 minutes. Add more water, 1 teaspoon at a time, if the mix isn't coming together. Too much water will make the dough wet.

3. Remove the dough from the food processor and set aside. You'll need the processor again for the filling, so there's no need to rinse or clean the container.

4. To make the filling, drain the raisins and cranberries, discard the soaking liquid, and add the drained dried fruit, almond butter, cinnamon, and salt to the food processor. Process continuously until a thick paste is achieved. Stop and scrape down the sides of the container to incorporate all the ingredients. Remove the filling from the container and set aside.

5. Rip off 2 large rectangular pieces of parchment paper. Shape the dough into a

(Continued on page 239)

Variations: Roll the cinnamon log in toasted coconut or hemp seeds before freezing for a different finish and added flavor.

ball and place in the middle of one of the pieces of parchment paper. Place the other piece of parchment paper on top of the dough and, using a rolling pin, roll out the dough into an 8 x 12-inch rectangle that's about ¼-inch thick. Do this by rolling from the center of the dough outward. Once you have approximately the right size and shape, use a knife to cut the dough into a neat rectangle and stick the cut-off pieces back into the dough and roll again as many times as needed to get a clean rectangle.

6. Spread the filling evenly over the dough, leaving ¼ inch of space around the edges.

7. Starting on the longest end, roll the dough over itself gently until your cinnamon roll log is formed. Keep the log on the parchment paper and place in the freezer on a level surface for 8 hours.

8. Once the cinnamon roll is firm, remove it from the freezer and place the log on a cutting board. Using a very sharp knife, slice the log into ¾-inch slices while the log is still frozen. Let the cinnamon rolls thaw for a few minutes before serving. Otherwise, lay them in a freezer-safe container (with parchment paper between each layer) and freeze for up to 3 months.

Chocolate Lover Brownies

Brownies—my weakness. I can barely be left alone with a freshly baked tray and no matter what, I always break my own baking rule and "accidentally" crumble off a corner as soon as they're out of the oven. These lightly sweetened, dense brownies are made from protein and fiber-rich beans. Paired with a creamy icing made from sweet potato, this treat is perfectly sweet, ooey, gooey, and satisfying. Whole-food dessert at its finest!

Makes 16 brownies

Ingredients

Brownie

½ cup gluten-free oat flour

½ cup + 2 tablespoons unsweetened cocoa powder

1 teaspoon baking powder

⅓ cup coconut sugar

¼ teaspoon cinnamon

¼ teaspoon sea salt

¼ cup cacao nibs, optional

2 tablespoons chia seeds

1½ cups cooked or canned chickpeas or black beans, drained and rinsed

1 medium, ripe banana

¼ cup well-stirred almond butter or preferred nut butter

⅓ cup maple syrup

¼ cup unsweetened almond or organic soy milk

2 teaspoons pure vanilla extract

Chocolate Sweet-Potato Icing

2 cups peeled and chopped sweet potato

¼ cup + 2 tablespoons maple syrup

⅓ cup unsweetened cocoa powder

⅛ teaspoon sea salt

Almond milk as needed

Optional Toppings

Cacao nibs, chopped almonds

Preparation

1. Position the oven rack in the middle of the oven and preheat to 350°F. Line an 8 x 8-inch square baking pan with parchment paper so that the parchment paper hangs out over two opposing sides.

2. In a large bowl, mix together the oat flour, cocoa powder, baking powder, coconut sugar, cinnamon, salt, and cacao nibs. Mix and set aside.

3. Add the chia seeds, beans, banana, almond butter, maple syrup, milk, and vanilla to a high-speed blender and blend until smooth.

4. Add the blended mixture to the dry ingredients and mix until no dry spots remain. Transfer the batter to the parchment-paper-lined pan and smooth out the surface. Bake the brownies for 20 to 22 minutes. The brownies are done when they're slightly firm.

5. Remove the brownies from the oven and let them cool completely in the pan. They'll continue to firm up as they cool.

6. While the brownies are cooking and cooling, make the icing. Steam the sweet potatoes in a small pot fitted with a steamer basket for 10 to 12 minutes or until very tender. Remove the sweet potatoes from the pot and let them cool.

(Continued on next page)

7. Add the cooled sweet potatoes, maple syrup, cocoa powder, and salt to a high-speed blender. Blend until completely smooth, using your tamper to help the blending. Add milk as needed, 1 tablespoon at a time, until the mixture is thick and smooth like icing. Transfer to a bowl and refrigerate until needed.

8. When the brownies have cooled, remove them from the pan by pulling up on the parchment paper and transfer them to a cutting board. Spread a thick layer of icing over the top. Garnish with chopped nuts or cacao nibs if desired.

9. Using a sharp knife, cut the brownies into 16 squares. Clean the knife between slices. Keep the brownies in the fridge for up to 3 days. You can freeze them, icing and all, for up to 3 months.

MENUS FOR ANY OCCASION

Birthday Dinner

Tahini Caesar with Quick Smoked
    Chickpeas & Bacon-ish Bits
Tuesday Tempeh Tacos
Black-Velvet Chocolate Cake

Summer BBQ

Strawberry Spinach Salads with
    White-Balsamic Dressing
The Summer Salad
B's Burgers with Sunflower
    Mozzarella
Mango Truffles

Holiday Party

Herbed Cheeze Ball
Warming Carrot & Tomato Soup
Market Shepherd's Pie
Carrot Cake & Citrus Cream-Cheese
    Icing
Mint Chocolate-Caramel Chews

Brunch

Sunshine Smoothies
All-Day Tofu Scramble
Banana-Raspberry Breakfast Bake
    Casserole

Valentine's Dinner

Sweet Potato Rosemary Bisque
Red Lentil Marinara Spaghetti
New York–Style Baked Chocolate-
    Swirl Cheesecake

INSPIRATION, EDUCATION & RESOURCES

I've learned a lot over the last ten years, and my teachings have come in all shapes and sizes. Yes, heaps and heaps of trial and error and digging into research and scientific papers, but my journey has been guided by many amazing people, and I want to point you in their direction so you can reap the benefits of their expertise and knowledge.

The Overcoming Multiple Sclerosis Charity (Overcomingms.org)
This charity, started by Dr. Jelinek (who also has multiple sclerosis), is centered on a seven-step, evidence-based approach to managing MS. The program dives deep into diet, exercise, stress management, vitamin D levels, and much more. This is where my journey with healing and lifestyle changes began. The free resources on this website and in the OMS book are incredibly helpful. If you or a family member has MS, please explore the OMS website and their reading materials. I'm also happy to say that all the recipes in this book are or can be made OMS friendly. To all my OMS-er friends, we're in this together and there are so many reasons to be hopeful! Thank you for your support over the years!

Forks Over Knives (forksoverknives.com)
I remember watching the documentary *Forks Over Knives*, created and produced by Brian Wendel, after I decided to adopt a plant-based lifestyle. I felt validated and armed with more knowledge! *Forks Over Knives: The Cookbook* was also the first plant-based cookbook I bought. Over the years I've contributed recipes, photography, and articles to Forks Over Knives, and I still suggest them as a number one resource for those choosing to transition to a plant-based diet. Their website has helpful educational materials including online cooking classes, and they now have a recipe-focused magazine as well.

The Physician's Committee for Responsible Medicine (PCRM.org)

PCRM is a nonprofit research and advocacy organization that promotes a plant-based diet and preventative medicine. Their website also has a helpful list of resources including a twenty-one-day kick-starter for a plant-based diet. Dr. Barnard has been a trusted resource of mine for almost a decade, and his commitment to cruelty-free, evidence-based health care is awe-inspiring. He has published several informative books and cookbooks.

Dr. Michael Greger and NutritionFacts.org

This is an online, science-based platform provided by Dr. Michael Greger and a dedicated team of professionals. They offer regular updates on nutritional science in the form of videos and easy-to-digest snippets. Dr. Greger's book *How Not to Die* is unrivaled in its depth and detail of plant-based nutritional research and recommendations. A highly recommended read as is his cookbook by the same name.

Cookbooks & Chefs

I've never met a cookbook I wasn't interested in. Really. I appreciate every type of cuisine, but I couldn't go without mentioning some of my favorites and those most influential in my culinary journey.

Amy Chaplin: author of James Beard Award–winning cookbook *At Home in the Whole Food Kitchen*, Amy is my idol. Her approach to food is refreshing and wholesome, and you'll learn so much from her work. I had tea with her once and it was magical.

Sarah Britton: It was Sarah who inspired me to investigate holistic nutrition. After reading her first cookbook *My New Roots* cover to cover, I knew I wanted to learn more about her approach to food and health. Her cookbooks are works of art!

Angela Liddon: Angela started a revolution. Simply put. Her first cookbook brought creative, plant-based cuisine to the masses. I was gifted this book for my thirtieth birthday while I was in culinary school and seeing her approach to food and recipe writing inspired me to keep going. *Oh She Glows* opened up many culinary doors for us health foodies.

To all the food bloggers and recipe developers turning whole foods into extraordinary culinary creations—you're changing how we eat one post and one recipe at a time, and your content matters! Thank you. I'll see you on the Interwebs.

Brands I Love

Artisana Organics: Raw nut and seed butters

Bobs Red Mill: Grain flours, arrowroot starch, almond flour, oats, dried beans, nutritional yeast, and grains and most gluten-free baking essentials

Banza: Chickpea pasta

Mara Natha: Raw and roasted nut butters

Eden Foods: Beans, tomato sauces, vinegars, tahini, tamari, BPA-free canned goods

Lundberg Family Farms: Whole grains, rice cakes, pasta

Simply Organic: Spices

Gogo Quinoa: Quinoa Flakes

Maison Orphée: Dijon mustard

Wholesome Sweeteners: Blackstrap molasses, coconut palm sugar

Manitoba Hemp: Hemp seeds

Mary's Gone Crackers: Whole-grain crackers

ACKNOWLEDGMENTS

First and foremost, Mom and Dad, Pam and George—I attribute everything good in my life to your support and love. Never questioning my path and always open to learning new things as I've reinvented myself over and over. Home is where you are, and I cannot thank you enough. I love you "all the monies in the world" and I miss you every day that I'm away.

Bernard—my chicken. Thank you for making every day joyful. Best friend, soulmate, all that eye-roll stuff, you are the bread to my almond butter. Thank you for being a bottomless pit and my biggest cheerleader.

My sisters, Penney and Pam, you've been there every step of the way, willing taste testers, and my regular consultants. I love you. Lily, my little soul sister, I see the signs of a chef in the making, I can't wait to create together!

To my testers. Thank you, *Thank you*! For dealing with my typos and random requests! Your feedback and comments were *essential* in creating these recipes. I have to give a special shout-out to a few for their commitment—Colleen, Patty, and Julie. I'm endlessly grateful for your time and energy.

Colleen, I could never thank you enough for being there for me in every one of my endeavors.

To the people who supported me in the beginning when I wasn't sure what I was doing. Jess, Colleen, Erin, Mom, Marg, Pammy, Penney. You came to my cooking classes, volunteered to be guinea pigs for whatever I was drumming up next, attended pop-ups and presentations. My heart is full. You, the people who are there in the beginning, when the finished product is rough, when the brand is not polished, you are the dream makers.

My moms—Marg and Pam. Thank you for the hours you devoted to me and my messy kitchen. I love you both.

Keely—thank you for your friendship, our inspiration-infused convos that keep me going! Ashley D, thank you for your amazing taste in design, feedback, and unwavering support during some weird and wonderful times.

Pete and Jess, thank you for your encouragement and always making me feel like my work is important. And listening to me talk about food and this cookbook ad nauseum!

To all my readers. Thank you for investing in my recipes and ideas, I hope this is the beginning of a long relationship.

A very special thank-you to Joanie Simon, from The Bite Shot. Without ever meeting and maybe without even knowing it, you generously offered your guidance and advice when it came to this monster of a photography project. You've helped turn my dreams into a reality.

To my editor, Nicole, thank you for your kind and patient communication and to Skyhorse Publishing, for taking a chance on an unknown author with big ideas.

Finally, Dustin Harder (multiple cookbook author and host of the Vegan Roadie web series)—I wanted to end this book where it began—with you. This cookbook would never have seen the light of day if you didn't believe in me. You found my book a home, without me even knowing it! Since that first day in culinary school when we sat together, I knew we'd be lifelong friends. I didn't know we'd be collaborators, confidants, and colleagues. Your enthusiasm and passion have helped me cultivate my own. Here's to many more years of creating alongside each other. From the bottom of my heart, thank you.

CONVERSION CHARTS

Measurement Equivalents

Cup	TBSP	TSP	Fluid OZ	Milliliter
1 C	16 Tbsp	48 tsp	8 oz	237 ml
¾ C	12 Tbsp	36 tsp	6 oz	177 ml
⅔ C	10 Tbsp + 2 tsp	32 tsp	5⅓ oz	158 ml
½ C	8 Tbsp	24 tsp	4 oz	118 ml
⅓ C	5 Tbsp + 1 tsp	16 tsp	2⅔ oz	79 ml
¼ C	4 Tbsp	12 tsp	2 oz	59 ml
⅙ C	2 Tbsp + 2 tsp	8 tsp	1⅓ oz	40 ml
⅛ C	2 Tbsp	6 tsp	1 oz	30 ml
¹⁄₁₆ C	1 Tbsp	3 tsp	½ oz	15 ml

Oven Temperatures

Fahrenheit	Celsius	Gas Mark
225°	110°	¼
250°	120°	½
275°	140°	1
300°	150°	2
325°	160°	3
350°	180°	4
375°	190°	5
400°	200°	6
425°	220°	7
450°	230°	8

INDEX

A

acorn squash, 93
All-Day Tofu Scramble, 54–55
almond butter, 18, 38, 41, 51, 52, 64, 72, 103, 125, 135, 209, 213, 217, 237, 241
almond flour, 15, 67, 72, 75, 217, 219, 225, 229, 235
almond meal, 15–16
almond milk, 37, 41, 42, 45, 51, 52, 56
almonds
  Almond Butter Caramel, 44–46
  Almond Milk, 48
  Apple, Almond & Chickpea Muffins, 64–65
  Bacon-ish Bits, 116–117
  Banana-Raspberry Breakfast Bake Casserole, 76–77
  Cashew Turmeric Parmesan, 148–149
  Cinnamon-Spiced House Granola, 47–48, 49
  Classic Almond Parmesan, 148–149
  Hickory Almond Parmesan, 148–149
  Raw Cinnamon Rolls, 237–239
  recipe ingredient, 18, 86, 123, 125
  Romesco Sauce, 191–193
anti-inflammatory diet, 1, 18, 19, 149, 169, 176, 214
antioxidants, 19, 51, 85, 185
apple cider vinegar, 20, 32, 45, 69, 75, 97, 113, 140, 175, 180, 189
apples
  Apple, Almond & Chickpea Muffins, 64–65
  Easy Apple-Berry Crumble, 212–213
  Warm Harvest Salad with Walnut Dressing, 108–109
applesauce, 48, 64, 217, 219, 229
Apricot, Cardamom & Blueberry Bars, 62–63

aquafaba, 28, 129, 132, 136, 139, 143
arrowroot starch, 16, 45, 75, 183, 199, 209, 213, 217, 225, 231
Artisana Organics, 249
arugula, 155, 171
Asian dishes
  Chinese "Fried" Quinoa, 164–165
  Pad Thai Protein Salad, 124–125
  Soothing Winter Squash & Miso Stew, 92–93
  Thai Curry Noodle Soup, 90–91
At Home in the Whole Food Kitchen (Chaplin), 248
avocado
  All-Day Tofu Scramble, 54–55
  Avocado Tartare, 130–131
  Chickpea & Avocado Savory Pancakes, 56–57
  Chickpea Smash Lettuce Cups, 160–161
  Fiesta Burrito Bowls, 178–179
  Pesto, 196–197
  The Summer Salad, 110–111
  Tuesday Tempeh Tacos, 150–151

B

B vitamins, 4, 155
baby arugula, 157
baby spinach
  recipe ingredient, 55, 89, 93, 100, 103, 152, 155, 162, 179, 197
  Rise n' Shine Smoothie Bowl, 38–39
  Strawberry Spinach Salad with White-Balsamic Dressing, 122–123
  The Summer Salad, 110–111
  Vegetable Lasagna & Tofu Ricotta with House Marinara, 201–203
Bacon-ish Bits, 113, 116–117
bagels, 74–75

baked goods. see also Breakfast Bakery; Sweets & Treats
  baking notes, 60
  freezing, 30
baking, 24, 26, 30
balsamic vinegar
  Balsamic Tempeh & Brussels Sprouts Bowl, 174–175
  Creamy Hemp-Balsamic Dressing, 106–107
  pantry staple, 20
  recipe ingredient, 95, 113, 176, 180, 195, 204
  Strawberry Spinach Salad with White-Balsamic Dressing, 122–123
bananas
  Banana-Raspberry Breakfast Bake Casserole, 76–77
  Blueberry, Banana & Chia Muffins, 72–73
  recipe ingredient, 38, 41, 42, 45, 52, 241
Banza, 249
Bars and Squares
  Apricot, Cardamom & Blueberry Bars, 62–63
  Country Date Squares, 219–221
  Pumpkin Pie Squares, 216–218
basil, 157, 196–197
BBQ Sauce, 180–181
BBQ Sheet-Pan Dinner, 180–181
beans
  consistency and temperature, 129
  cooking properly, 14, 27–28
  cooking tips, 29, 32
  in plant-based cooking, 5
beets
  The Blackout Burger, 185–187
  Brilliant Beet Hummus, 142–143
  Pink Quinoa & Cheezy Kale Bowl, 176–177
berries
  Easy Apple-Berry Crumble, 212–213

Everyday Overnight Oats,
36–37
Layered Berry Chia Pudding
& Creamy Oat Parfait,
52–53
Rise n' Shine Smoothie Bowl,
38
beta-carotene, 4, 51
binders, 15–16, 18, 19
black beans
Black Velvet Icing, *228–230*
The Blackout Burger, *185–187*
Chocolate Lover Brownies,
240–242
Fiesta Burrito Bowls, *178–179*
Loaded Lunch Salad, *106–107*
The Summer Salad, *110–111*
Tangy Roasted Red Pepper
& Black Bean Spread,
136–137
black olives, 119
black pepper, 169
black rice, 185, 187
blackstrap molasses, 217, 218,
225
Black-Velvet Chocolate Cake,
228–230
blenders, 11
blending, 24, 26
blood sugar, 3
blueberries
Apricot, Cardamom &
Blueberry Bars, *62–63*
Blueberry, Banana & Chia
Muffins, *72–73*
Everyday Overnight Oats,
36–37
Sunshine Smoothie, *42–43*
Bobs Red Mill, 249
boiling, 24
Bowl Meals
Balsamic Tempeh & Brussels
Sprouts Bowl, *174–175*
building a bowl, 167
Fiesta Burrito Bowls, *178–179*
Fresh Falafel & Tzatziki Bowl,
171–173
Golden Bowls, *168–170*
Pink Quinoa & Cheezy Kale
Bowl, 176–*177*
box grater, 12
bran, 5
brand recommendations, 249
breads
Amazing Multigrain Bread,
69–71
Mini Buckwheat bagels, *74–75*
Breakfast & Brunch

All-Day Tofu Scramble,
54–55
Banana-Raspberry Breakfast
Bake Casserole, 76–77
Butterm*lk Buckwheat
Pancakes with Almond
Butter Caramel, 44–46
Chickpea & Avocado Savory
Pancakes, 56–57
Cinnamon-Spiced House
Granola, 47–48, 49
Cozy Pumpkin Bowls, 50–51
Everyday Overnight Oats,
36–37
Layered Berry Chia Pudding
& Creamy Oat Parfait,
52–53
Raw Green Buckwheat Bowl,
40–41
Rise n' Shine Smoothie Bowl,
38–*39*
Sunshine Smoothie, *42–43*
Breakfast Bakery
Amazing Multigrain Bread,
69–71
Apple, Almond & Chickpea
Muffins, *64–65*
Apricot, Cardamom &
Blueberry Bars, *62–63*
baking notes, 60
Banana-Raspberry Breakfast
Bake Casserole, 76–77
Blueberry, Banana & Chia
Muffins, *72–73*
Cranberry-Orange Muffins
with Rosemary, *66, 67–68*
Mini Buckwheat bagels,
74–75
overview, 58
Brilliant Beet Hummus, *142–143*
Britton, Sarah, 248
broccoli
ingredient, 90, 107, 125
One-Pot Broccoli Hummus
Mac n' Cheeze, 206–207
Sweet & Sour Chickpea-
Stuffed Sweet Potatoes,
182–183
Vegetable Lasagna & Tofu
Ricotta with House
Marinara, 201–203
Weeknight Tempeh &
Vegetable Casserole,
208–209
broth, *80–81*
brown lentils, 199
brown rice, 4, 12–13, 93. *see also*
Rice Dishes

brown rice flour, 15, 45, 95, 185,
225
brown rice pasta, 90, 195, 197,
201, 207
brownies, *240–242*
brussels sprouts
Balsamic Tempeh & Brussels
Sprouts Bowl, *174–175*
Warm Harvest Salad with
Walnut Dressing, 108–*109*
B's Burger, 188–190
buckwheat
Amazing Multigrain Bread,
69–71
Butterm*lk Buckwheat
Pancakes with Almond
Butter Caramel, 44–46
Mini Buckwheat bagels,
74–75
in plant-based cooking, 4, 13
Raw Green Buckwheat Bowl,
40–41
buckwheat flour, 15, 45, 75
Burgers
The Blackout Burger, 185–187
B's Burger, 188–190
freezing, 29
burrito bowl, *178–179*
Butterm*lk Buckwheat
Pancakes with Almond
Butter Caramel, *44–46*
butternut squash
Lentil Butternut Squash
Stew, *102–103*
Soothing Winter Squash &
Miso Stew, *92–93*

C
cabbage, 107, 125
cacao nibs, 241
Cakes
Black-Velvet Chocolate Cake,
228–230
Carrot Cake & Citrus Cream-
Cheese Icing, *234–236*
calorie density, 3
Campari tomatoes, 119, 171
canned/bottled food, 20, 28, 85,
129, 204
cannellini beans, 140–*141*
capers, 20, 113, 132, 157
caramel, *44–46, 222–223*
cardamom, *62–63*
carrots
Carrot Cake & Citrus Cream-
Cheese Icing, *234–236*
Homemade Vegetable Broth,
80–81

ingredient, 89, 93, 95, 100, 103, 107, 125, 162, 171, 195, 199, 201, 209
Spiced Creamy Carrot Hummus, *138*–139
Warming Carrot & Tomato Soup, *84*–85
cashews
cashew cream, 86
Cashew Turmeric Parmesan, *148*–149, 176
Citrus Cream-Cheese Icing, *234*–236
Date & Dijon Sauce, *174*–175
Herbed Cheeze Ball, 144–*145*
Mango Truffles, 226–*227*
New York-Style Baked Chocolate-Swirl Cheesecake, 231–233
Sour Cream, 97
Sunflower Mozzarella, 157–159
as thickener, 90
Tzatziki, 171–173
Unforgettable French Onion Dip, 140–*141*
cauliflower
BBQ Sheet-Pan Dinner, 180–*181*
Cauliflower Potato Dal, *152*–153
Creamy Romesco & Roasted Cauliflower Penne, 191–193
Golden Bowls, *168*–170
Golden Garlic & Cauliflower Soup, 82–*83*
Loaded Lunch Salad, *106*–107
Market Shepherd's Pie, *198*–200
celery, *80*–81, 89, 95, 100, 103, 108, 161, 162, 165, 199
Chaplin, Amy, 248
Cheese alternatives
Cheezy Hummus Sauce, *206*–207
Cheezy Kale, 176–*177*
Citrus Cream-Cheese Icing, *234*–236
Herbed Cheeze Ball, 144–*145*
New York-Style Baked Chocolate-Swirl Cheesecake, 231–233
The Parmesans, *148*–149, 176
Sun-Dried Tomato Tofu Feta, *118*–120
Sunflower Mozzarella, 157–159

Tofu Ricotta, 201
Unforgettable French Onion Dip, 140–*141*
cheesecake, 231–233
cherry tomatoes, 97–99, 107, 111, 157, 169
chewing, 38, 42
chia seeds
Blueberry, Banana & Chia Muffins, 72–*73*
Everyday Overnight Oats, *36*–37
ingredient, 45, 75, 214, 226, 241
Layered Berry Chia Pudding & Creamy Oat Parfait, *52*–53
in plant-based cooking, 18–19
chickpea flour, 22, 56
chickpea miso, 17
chickpeas
Apple, Almond & Chickpea Muffins, 64–*65*
BBQ Sheet-Pan Dinner, 180–*181*
Brilliant Beet Hummus, *142*–143
B's Burger, 188–190
Cheezy Hummus Sauce, *206*–207
Chickpea & Avocado Savory Pancakes, 56–*57*
Chickpea Smash Lettuce Cups, *160*–161
Chocolate Lover Brownies, *240*–242
Fresh Falafel & Tzatziki Bowl, 171–173
Loaded Lunch Salad, *106*–107
Our House Hummus, *132*–133
Quick Pickled Cucumber Side Salad with Chickpeas, *126*–127
Smoky Chickpea Stew with Cherry Tomatoes & Kale, 97–99
Spiced Creamy Carrot Hummus, *138*–139
Sweet & Sour Chickpea-Stuffed Sweet Potatoes, *182*–184
Tahini Caesar with Quick Smoked Chickpeas & Bacon-ish Bits, *112*–114
chilis, 90, 136
Chinese "Fried" Quinoa, *164*–165

chocolate
Black-Velvet Chocolate Cake, *228*–230
Chocolate Lover Brownies, *240*–242
Mint Chocolate-Caramel Chews, 222–*223*
New York-Style Baked Chocolate-Swirl Cheesecake, 231–233
cholesterol, 3, 4, 5
chronic disease, xiv, 7, 8
chronic inflammation, 1
cinnamon rolls, 237
Cinnamon-Spiced House Granola, *47*–48
Citrus Cream-Cheese Icing, *234*–236
citrus juices, 19–20, 32
Classic Almond Parmesan, *148*–149
Cleansing Turnip & Fennel Soup, *88*–89
cocoa powder, 222–*223*, 229, 231, 241
coconut, 214, 226
coconut aminos, 20
coconut oil, 7
coconut sugar, 22, 63, 64, 113, 189, 195, 204, 209, 213, 217, 225, 229, 231, 235, 241
Condiments. *see also* Salad Dressings; Sauces
BBQ Sauce, 180–*181*
cashew cream, 86
Sour Cream, 97
cookbooks/chefs, 248
cookies, *224*–225
cooking methods
basic techniques
baking, 24, 26
blend/process, 24, 26
boiling, 24
sauté, 25
simmering, 25
soaking, 21, 24, 25, 27–28, 41
steaming, 24
cooking grains
flavoring, 27
simple method, 26
soaking, 27–28
toasting, 27
cooking legumes, 27–28
oil-free cooking, 6–7, 25–26
cooking tips
batch grains and beans, 29
cashew cream, 86

chop first, 30
dried herbs, 108
freezing foods, 29
grinding spices, 100
icing cakes, 230
multiple meals, 30
notes for all recipes, 32
pancakes, 46
reheating muffins, 68
roasting beets, 143
roasting garlic, 82
roasting red peppers, 193
sauces, 29
saving tomato paste, 99
season last, 30
cooling baked goods, 60
corn, 179
Coscarelli, Chloe, xvi
Cozy Pumpkin Bowls, 50–51
cranberries
Country Date Squares, 219–221
Cranberry-Orange Muffins with Rosemary, 66, 67–68
ingredient, 108, 237
Cranberry-Orange Muffins with Rosemary, 66, 67–68
Creamy Hemp-Balsamic Dressing, 106–107
creamy hummus, 129
crust recipes, 216–218, 219–221, 231
cucumbers
Avocado Tartare, 130–131
ingredient, 107, 119, 125, 127
Tzatziki, 171–173
curry powder, 89

D
dal, 152
dates
Almond Butter Caramel, 45
BBQ Sauce, 180–181
Black Velvet Icing, 228–230
Country Date Squares, 219–221
Date & Dijon Sauce, 174–175
Lemon-Turmeric Bliss Balls, 214–215
Mint Chocolate-Caramel Chews, 222–223
Pumpkin Pie Squares, 216–218
Raw Cinnamon Rolls, 237–239
soaking, 21
as sweetener, 21, 41, 51, 107
desserts. see Sweets & Treats

Dijon mustard, 55, 97, 107, 108, 113, 123, 155, 161, 174–175, 180, 199, 207, 249
dill, 127, 131, 171, 182–184
dill pickles, 161
Dips and Spreads
Avocado Tartare, 130–131
Brilliant Beet Hummus, 142–143
cooking tips, 129
Herbed Cheeze Ball, 144–145
Our House Hummus, 132–133
overview, 129
Spiced Creamy Carrot Hummus, 138–139
Spring Edamame Green-Pea Hummus, 134–135
Tangy Roasted Red Pepper & Black Bean Spread, 136–137
Tzatziki, 171–173
Unforgettable French Onion Dip, 140–141
dishers/spring-released scoops, 11–12, 46, 225
donut pans, 75
dried fruit, 21, 48, 62–63, 64, 161, 226–227, 237
dried herbs, 108
dulse flakes, 22

E
"eat the rainbow," 4, 125
edamame
Pad Thai Protein Salad, 124–125
pantry staple, 17–18
Spring Edamame Green-Pea Hummus, 134–135
Eden Foods, 249
egg-replacers, 15–16, 19
"empty calories," 3
endosperm, 5
English cucumbers, 127. see also cucumbers
essential fatty acids, 7, 18, 42
Everyday Overnight Oats, 36–37
extra-firm and firm tofu, 17. see also tofu

F
fat, 5, 7
fennel, 88–89
fiber, 3, 4, 15, 16, 19, 21, 22, 63, 72, 96, 155, 241
Fiesta Burrito Bowls, 178–179
fine-mesh strainer, 12
flax seeds, 18, 19, 38, 237

flax seeds, ground, 41, 42, 52, 171, 189, 219
flours & baking
almond flour, 15
arrowroot starch, 16
brand recommendations, 249
brown rice flour, 15
buckwheat flour, 15
gluten-free, 14
oat flour, 15
psyllium husk, 15–16
soy products, 16–17
food, and health, xiv–xv, xvi, 6
food philosophy, 1–9
gluten-free, 7–8
imperfection, 9
no/low-oil cooking, 6–7
plant-based whole foods, 3–6
processed foods vs whole foods, 6, 7
recipe creation, 1–3
vegan, 7
food processors, 11, 24
Forks Over Knives, 247
fried "rice," 164–165
fruit, 4, 21

G
garlic
Golden Garlic & Cauliflower Soup, 82–83
Homemade Vegetable Broth, 80–81
ingredient, 81, 85, 86, 89, 90, 93, 95, 97, 100, 103, 113, 127, 131, 132, 135, 139, 143, 152, 155, 157, 161, 162, 165, 171, 175, 179, 183, 185, 191, 195, 197, 199, 204, 207
roasting, 82
germ, grain, 5
ginger, 42, 82, 85, 90, 93, 100, 103, 125, 183, 209, 225
Gingerbread Cloud Cookies, 224–225
gluten-free diet, 8–9, 13, 14
Gogo Quinoa, 249
Golden Bowls, 168–170
granola, 47–48, 49
gravy, 154–156
Greek Salad with Sun-Dried-Tomato Tofu Feta, 118–120
green peas
Chinese "Fried" Quinoa, 164–165
Market Shepherd's Pie, 199
One-Pot Broccoli Hummus Mac n' Cheeze, 206–207

Perfect Green-Pea Pesto Pasta, *196–197*
Spring Edamame Green-Pea Hummus, *134*–135
Vegetable Jambalaya, *162–163*
Greger, Michael, 248

H
Health Canada, 3
hemp seeds, 18, 38, 42, 64, *106*–107, 125, 214, 226, 249
Herbed Cheeze Ball, 144–*145*
Herbed Sunflower Dressing, *118*–120
herbs & spices, 19, 81, 108
Hickory Almond Parmesan, *148*–149
Himalayan salt, 23
holistic nutrition, xv
Homemade Vegetable Broth, *80*–81
hot sauce, 125, 183, 209
House Marinara, 204–*205*
How Not to Die (Greger), 248
Hummus
Brilliant Beet Hummus, *142–143*
Cheezy Hummus Sauce, *206–207*
Our House Hummus, *132–133*
Spiced Creamy Carrot Hummus, *138–139*
Spring Edamame Green-Pea Hummus, *134*–135

I
Icings
Black Velvet Icing, *228*–230
Chocolate Sweet Potato Icing, *240–242*
Citrus Cream-Cheese Icing, *234–236*
imperfection, 9
In Defense of Food (Pollan), x
Indian Black Salt, 23, 55
Indian dishes
Cauliflower Potato Dal, 152–*153*
Indian Split Pea Soup, 100–*101*
inflammation, 1, 6–7, 8, 42
International flavors
Cauliflower Potato Dal, 152–*153*
Chinese "Fried" Quinoa, *164–165*

Creamy Romesco & Roasted Cauliflower Penne, 191–193
Fiesta Burrito Bowls, *178–179*
Indian Split Pea Soup, 100–*101*
Pad Thai Protein Salad, *124*–125
Soothing Winter Squash & Miso Stew, *92–93*
Thai Curry Noodle Soup, 90–*91*
Tuesday Tempeh Tacos, *150*–151
iodine, 22
iron, 4, 16, 18, 103

J
jalapeño peppers, 151, 179
julienne peeler, 12

K
kabocha, 93
Kala Namak, 23, 55
kale
ingredient, 42, 55, 89, 93, 100, 152, 162, 169, 179, 183, 197
Pink Quinoa & Cheezy Kale Bowl, 176–*177*
Smoky Chickpea Stew with Cherry Tomatoes & Kale, 97–99
Tahini Caesar with Quick Smoked Chickpeas & Bacon-ish Bits, *112–114*
kasha, 13
kombu, 22, 28, 81

L
lasagna, 201–203
Layered Berry Chia Pudding & Creamy Oat Parfait, 52–*53*
leafy greens. *see* Salads
legumes, 5, 14, 27–28, 152
lemon juice/zest, 20, 45, 55, 56, 82, 85, 86, 89, 100, 103, 113, 119, 132, 135, 139, 140, 143, 144, 152, 161, 169, 171, 176, 183, 197, 201, 207, 231
lemongrass, 90
Lemon-Turmeric Bliss Balls, *214–215*
lentils
Cauliflower Potato Dal, 152–*153*
cooking tips, 27
Lentil Butternut Squash Stew, 102–103

Loaded Lunch Salad, *106–107*
Market Shepherd's Pie, *198–200*
pantry staple, 5, 14
Red Lentil Marinara Spaghetti, 194–195
Liddon, Angela, 248
lime juice/zest, 20, 90, *110*–111, 131, 136, 151, 179
liquid aminos, 20
Loaded Lunch Salad, *106–107*
Lundberg Family Farms, 249
lycopene, 4, 85

M
magnesium, 4, 18
Main Meals. *see also* Bowl Meals; Burgers; Pasta
BBQ Sheet-Pan Dinner, 180–*181*
Cauliflower Potato Dal, 152–*153*
Chickpea Smash Lettuce Cups, *160*–161
Market Shepherd's Pie, *198–200*
Rustic Mashed Potatoes & Mushroom-Miso Gravy, *154–156*
Sweet & Sour Chickpea-Stuffed Sweet Potatoes, *182–184*
Weeknight Tempeh & Vegetable Casserole, *208–209*
Maison Orphée, 249
mango
Avocado Tartare, *130–131*
Mango Truffles, 226–*227*
Rise n' Shine Smoothie Bowl, *38–39*
The Summer Salad, *110*–111
Manitoba Hemp, 249
maple syrup, 7, 21, 41, 48, 52, 72, 76, 108, 113, 169, 171, 175, 213, 219, 226, 229, 231, *234*–236, 241
marinades, tofu, 55, 95, 119, 120, 175
Market Shepherd's Pie, *198–200*
Mary's Gone Crackers, 249
measuring ingredients, 60
Meat alternatives
The Blackout Burger, 185–187
B's Burger, 188–190
Fiesta Burrito Bowls, *178–179*
Market Shepherd's Pie, *198–200*

Tuesday Tempeh Tacos, *150–151*
Vegetable Jambalaya, *162–163*
medicine, xiv, xv
menu suggestions, 245
Mexican flavors
    Fiesta Burrito Bowls, *178–179*
    Tuesday Tempeh Tacos, *150–151*
microplanes, 12
minerals, 22, 23, 218
Mini Buckwheat bagels, *74–75*
Mint Chocolate-Caramel Chews, *222–223*
miso, 17, 93, 139, 144, 155, 189, 197, 199, 201
molasses, 217, 218, 225
MS diagnosis, author's, x, xiii–xiv, 7, 247
Muffins
    Apple, Almond & Chickpea Muffins, *64–65*
    Blueberry, Banana & Chia Muffins, *72–73*
    Cranberry-Orange Muffins with Rosemary, 66, *67–68*
    freezing, 29
    reheating, 68
mushrooms
    B's Burger, *188–190*
    Chinese "Fried" Quinoa, *164–165*
    ingredient, 55, 81, 90, 93, 151, 195, 199
    Portobello Pizzas with Sunflower Mozzarella, *157–159*
    Rustic Mashed Potatoes & Mushroom-Miso Gravy, *154–156*
    Vegetable Lasagna & Tofu Ricotta with House Marinara, 201–203
My New Roots (Britton), 248

N
Natural Gourmet Institute, xv
navy beans
    Rustic Mashed Potatoes & Mushroom-Miso Gravy, *154–156*
    Soothing Winter Squash & Miso Stew, *92–93*
    Spiced Creamy Carrot Hummus, *138–139*
    Unforgettable French Onion Dip, 140–*141*

New York-Style Baked Chocolate-Swirl Cheesecake, 231–233
nonstick sauté pan, 12
noodles, 90–*91*
notes for all recipes, 32
nourish bowls. *see* Bowl Meals
nut milks, 48
nut-milk bag, 12
nutrient density, 3, 5, 96
nutritional yeast, 22, 55, 56, 97, 113, 116, 144, 149, 155, 169, 171, 189, 197, 199, 201, 207
NutritionFacts.org, 248
nuts & seeds, 5, 17, 107

O
oat flour, 15, 63, 64, 72, 171, 217, 219, 229, 235, 241
Oh She Glows (Liddon), 248
oil-free cooking, 6–7, 25–26, 46
oils, 1–2, 6–7, 25–26
olives, 119
omega-3 fats, 18, 19, 72
omega-6 fats, 6–7, 18
One-Pot Broccoli Hummus Mac n' Cheeze, *206–207*
onions
    Homemade Vegetable Broth, *80–81*
    ingredient, 55, 82, 85, 86, 89, 90, 93, 95, 97, 100, 103, 111, 162, 165, 189, 195, 199, 207, 209
    Unforgettable French Onion Dip, 140–*141*
orange juice/zest
    Citrus Cream-Cheese Icing, *234–236*
    Cranberry-Orange Muffins with Rosemary, 66, *67–68*
    ingredient, 20, 51, 63, 107, 209, 219, 225
Our House Hummus, 132–*133*
Overcoming Multiple Sclerosis (OMS), 247
overnight oats, 36–37, 52–*53*

P
Pad Thai Protein Salad, *124–125*
pancakes, *44–46*, 56–*57*
parchment paper, 60
pasta
    Creamy Romesco & Roasted Cauliflower Penne, 191–193
    One-Pot Broccoli Hummus Mac n' Cheeze, *206–207*

Perfect Green-Pea Pesto Pasta, *196–197*
    in plant-based cooking, 9, 18
    Vegetable Lasagna & Tofu Ricotta with House Marinara, 201–203
peanuts, 5
penne, 191–193
peppermint extract, 222
Perfect Green-Pea Pesto Pasta, *196–197*
pesto, *196–197*
phytonutrients, 4, 19, 41, 67, 169
pickles, *126–127*, 161
pineapple, 42
Pink Himalayan salt, 23, 32
Pink Quinoa & Cheezy Kale Bowl, 176–*177*
pizza, 157–159
plant-based diet, 8
plant-based food groups
    legumes, 5
    nuts & seeds, 5
    vegetables & fruit, 4
    whole grains, 4–5
plant-based kitchen
    overview, x–xi, 2
    pantry
        canned/bottled food, 20
        flours & baking, 14–16
        herbs & spices, 19
        legumes, 14
        miscellaneous ingredients, 22–23
        nuts & seeds, 18
        pasta, 18
        super seeds, 18–19
        sweeteners, 21–22
        vinegars, citrus & seasonings, 19
        whole grains, 12–13
    tools, 11–12
Pollan, Michael, x
Portobello Pizzas with Sunflower Mozzarella, 157–159
potassium, 155
potatoes
    All-Day Tofu Scramble, *54–55*
    BBQ Sheet-Pan Dinner, 180–*181*
    Cauliflower Potato Dal, 152–*153*
    Market Shepherd's Pie, *198–200*
    peel nutrients, 96

Rustic Mashed Potatoes &
　　Mushroom-Miso Gravy,
　　154–156
Smoky Chickpea Stew with
　　Cherry Tomatoes & Kale,
　　97–99
Sunday Tempeh Stew, *94*–96
power bowls. *see* Bowl Meals
probiotics, 16, 20
processed foods, 6, 7, 22
protein, 13, 16, 18, 22, 63, *124*–125,
　　167, 169, 241
psyllium husk, 15–16, 63, 67, 69,
　　75, 76, 219, 229, 231, 235
pulses (legumes), 5
pumpkin
　　Cozy Pumpkin Bowls, *50*–51
　　Pumpkin Pie Squares,
　　　216–218
pumpkin seeds, 169, 189, 190

Q
Quick Pickled Cucumber
　　Side Salad with Chickpeas,
　　126–127
quinoa. *see also* pasta
　　Amazing Multigrain Bread,
　　　69–71
　　Chinese "Fried" Quinoa,
　　　164–165
　　Fresh Falafel & Tzatziki Bowl,
　　　171–173
　　Golden Bowls, *168*–170
　　Loaded Lunch Salad, *106*–107
　　Pad Thai Protein Salad,
　　　124–125
　　Pink Quinoa & Cheezy Kale
　　　Bowl, 176–*177*
　　in plant-based cooking, 4,
　　　9, 13
　　The Summer Salad, *110*–111
quinoa flakes, 63, 249
quinoa pasta, 195, 197

R
raisins, 64, 235
raspberries
　　Banana-Raspberry Breakfast
　　　Bake Casserole, 76–77
　　Everyday Overnight Oats,
　　　36–37
Raw Cinnamon Rolls, 237–239
Raw Green Buckwheat Bowl,
　　40–41
red bell peppers, 90, 111, 125, 151,
　　161, 162, 165, 179, 180, 189
red lentils, 14, 152–*153*, *194*–195.
　　see also lentils

red onion, 119, 123, 127, 131, 152,
　　179, 183, 185, 201, 204
refined grains, 4, 5
reheating muffins, 68
resources, 247–248
Rice Dishes
　　Balsamic Tempeh & Brussels
　　　Sprouts Bowl, *174*–175
　　Fiesta Burrito Bowls, *178*–179
　　Golden Bowls, *168*–170
　　Herbed Rice, *174*–175
　　The Summer Salad, *110*–111
　　Vegetable Jambalaya,
　　　162–*163*
　　Warm Harvest Salad with
　　　Walnut Dressing, 108–*109*
　　Weeknight Tempeh &
　　　Vegetable Casserole,
　　　208–209
rice wine vinegar, 20, 125, 127, 209
Rise n' Shine Smoothie Bowl,
　　38–*39*
RiseShineCook.ca, xvi, 38
roasted red pepper
　　Creamy Romesco & Roasted
　　　Cauliflower Penne,
　　　191–193
　　roasting red peppers, 193
　　Tangy Roasted Red Pepper
　　　& Black Bean Spread,
　　　136–*137*
roasting tips, 82, 193
rolled oats
　　Amazing Multigrain Bread,
　　　69–71
　　Apricot, Cardamom &
　　　Blueberry Bars, 63
　　Banana-Raspberry Breakfast
　　　Bake Casserole, 76–77
　　The Blackout Burger, 185–187
　　Blueberry, Banana & Chia
　　　Muffins, 72–*73*
　　B's Burger, 188–190
　　cheesecake crust, 231
　　Cinnamon-Spiced House
　　　Granola, *47*–48, *49*
　　Country Date Squares,
　　　219–221
　　Cozy Pumpkin Bowls, 51
　　Cranberry-Orange Muffins
　　　with Rosemary, *66*, 67–68
　　Easy Apple-Berry Crumble,
　　　212–213
　　Everyday Overnight Oats,
　　　36–37
　　Layered Berry Chia Pudding
　　　& Creamy Oat Parfait,
　　　52–*53*

Lemon-Turmeric Bliss Balls,
　　214–*215*
Mango Truffles, 226–*227*
pantry staple, 13
Raw Cinnamon Rolls,
　　237–239
Warming Carrot & Tomato
　　Soup, 84–85
romaine lettuce
　　Chickpea Smash Lettuce
　　　Cups, *160*–161
　　Greek Salad with Sun-
　　　Dried-Tomato Tofu Feta,
　　　118–120
　　Tahini Caesar with Quick
　　　Smoked Chickpeas &
　　　Bacon-ish Bits, *112*–114
Romesco Sauce, 191–193
rosemary
　　Cranberry-Orange Muffins
　　　with Rosemary, *66*–68
　　Sweet Potato Rosemary
　　　Bisque, 86–*87*

S
Salad Dressings
　　Creamy Hemp-Balsamic
　　　Dressing, *106*–107
　　Herbed Sunflower Dressing,
　　　118–120
　　oil-free cooking, 26
　　Pad Thai Sauce, *124*–125
　　Strawberry Spinach Salad
　　　with White-Balsamic
　　　Dressing, *122*–123
　　Tahini Caesar Dressing,
　　　112–114
　　Walnut Dressing, 108–*109*
Salads
　　Bacon-ish Bits, 116–*117*
　　Greek Salad with Sun-Dried-
　　　Tomato Tofu Feta, *118*–120
　　Loaded Lunch Salad with
　　　Creamy Hemp-Balsamic
　　　Dressing, *106*–107
　　overview, 104
　　Pad Thai Protein Salad,
　　　124–125
　　Quick Pickled Cucumber
　　　Side Salad with
　　　Chickpeas, *126*–127
　　Strawberry Spinach Salad
　　　with White-Balsamic
　　　Dressing, *122*–123
　　The Summer Salad, *110*–111
　　Tahini Caesar with Quick
　　　Smoked Chickpeas &
　　　Bacon-ish Bits, *112*–113

Warm Harvest Salad with
    Walnut Dressing, 108–*109*
salt, 22–23, 32
saturated fat, 7
Sauces. *see also* Salad Dressings
    Almond Butter Caramel,
      44–46
    BBQ Sauce, 180–*181*
    binders, 19
    building a bowl, 167
    Cheezy Hummus Sauce,
      206–207
    Date & Dijon Sauce, *174*–175
    Golden Tahini Sauce,
      168–170
    House Marinara, 204–*205*
    keeping on hand, 29
    Mushroom-Miso Gravy,
      154–156
    oil-free cooking, 26
    Pad Thai Sauce, *124*–125
    Pesto, *196*–197
    Romesco Sauce, 191–193
    Tahini Caesar Dressing,
      112–114
    Tahini Dill Sauce, *182*–184
    Tzatziki, 171–173
sauté cooking method, 25–26
savory pancakes, 56–*57*
seasonings, 19–20, 30, 32,
    148–149
seaweed, 22
sesame seeds, 75, 149, 165, 214
sheet-pan dinner, 180–*181*
shepherd's pie, *198*–200
shoyu, 9, 20
silicone baking pans, 12, 60
silken tofu, 17
simmering, 25
Simply Organic, 249
slurry, 16
Smoky Chickpea Stew with
    Cherry Tomatoes & Kale,
    97–99
smoothie bowls, 38–*39*
smoothies, 42–*43*
soaking
    cooking method, 24, 25
    dates, 21
    grains, 27, 41
    legumes, 27–28
soaking cooking method, 21, 25
sodium, 19, 20, 22–23
soluble fiber, 15
Soothing Winter Squash & Miso
    Stew, 92–*93*
Soups. *see also* Stews

Cleansing Turnip & Fennel
    Soup, *88*–89
freezing, 29
Golden Garlic & Cauliflower
    Soup, 82–*83*
Homemade Vegetable Broth,
    80–81
Indian Split Pea Soup,
    100–*101*
overview, 79
Sweet Potato Rosemary
    Bisque, 86–*87*
Thai Curry Noodle Soup,
    90–*91*
Warming Carrot & Tomato
    Soup, 84–85
Sour Cream, 97
soy products
    edamame, 17–18
    extra-firm and firm tofu, 17
    miso, 17
    silken tofu, 17
    tamari, 9, 20
    tempeh, 16–17
soy sauce, 9, 20
soybeans, 5
Spiced Creamy Carrot
    Hummus, *138*–139
spices, 32, 100, 165, 249
spinach, 42, 56, 183. *see also*
    baby spinach
spiralizers, 12
split peas
    cooking tips, 27
    Indian Split Pea Soup,
      100–*101*
    pantry staple, 5, 14
Spring Edamame Green-Pea
    Hummus, *134*–135
squash
    Lentil Butternut Squash
      Stew, *102*–103
    Soothing Winter Squash &
      Miso Stew, 92–*93*
steaming, 24–25
steaming basket, 12
Stews. *see also* Soups
    Lentil Butternut Squash
      Stew, *102*–103
    overview, 79
    Smoky Chickpea Stew with
      Cherry Tomatoes & Kale,
      97–99
    Soothing Winter Squash &
      Miso Stew, 92–*93*
    Sunday Tempeh Stew, *94*–96
stir-fry cooking method, 25
storing food

almond flour, 15
freezing foods, 29–30
herbs, 19
nuts, 5
oat flour, 15
strawberry spinach salad,
    122–123
Sunday Tempeh Stew, *94*–96
sun-dried tomatoes, *118*–120
sunflower seeds
    Bacon-ish Bits, 116–*117*
    cheesecake crust, 231
    Herbed Sunflower Dressing,
      118–120
    Sunflower Mozzarella,
      157–159
Sunshine Smoothie, 42–*43*
super seeds
    chia, 18–19
    flax, 18, 19
    hemp, 18
sweet potatoes
    BBQ Sheet-Pan Dinner,
      180–*181*
    Chocolate Sweet Potato
      Icing, 240–242
    Indian Split Pea Soup,
      100–*101*
    Market Shepherd's Pie, 199
    Pad Thai Protein Salad,
      124–125
    Sweet & Sour Chickpea-
      Stuffed Sweet Potatoes,
      182–184
    Sweet Potato Rosemary
      Bisque, 86–*87*
    Warm Harvest Salad with
      Walnut Dressing, 108–*109*
sweeteners, 21, 22, 42, 60, 218,
    249
Sweets & Treats
    Almond Butter Caramel,
      44–46
    Black-Velvet Chocolate Cake,
      228–230
    Carrot Cake & Citrus Cream-
      Cheese Icing, *234–236*
    Chocolate Lover Brownies,
      240–242
    Country Date Squares,
      219–221
    Easy Apple-Berry Crumble,
      212–213
    Gingerbread Cloud Cookies,
      224–225
    Lemon-Turmeric Bliss Balls,
      214–*215*
    Mango Truffles, 226–*227*

Mint Chocolate-Caramel
Chews, 222–*223*
New York-Style Baked
Chocolate-Swirl
Cheesecake, 231–233
overview, 211
Pumpkin Pie Squares,
216–218
Raw Cinnamon Rolls,
237–239
Swiss chard, 93, 100, 183

T
tacos, *150*–151
tahini
Golden Tahini Sauce,
168–170
ingredient, 18, 67, 82, 123, 132,
139, 143, 199, 201, 226
Tahini Caesar Dressing,
112–114
Tahini Dill Sauce, *182*–184
Tahini Caesar with Quick
Smoked Chickpeas & Bacon-
ish Bits, *112*–114
tamari, 9, 20, 32, 90, 93, 95, 103,
107, 113, 119, 125, 155, 157, 162,
175, 180, 183, 199, 207, 209
Tangy Roasted Red Pepper &
Black Bean Spread, 136–*137*
tempeh
Balsamic Tempeh & Brussels
Sprouts Bowl, *174*–175
pantry staple, 16–17
Sunday Tempeh Stew, *94*–96
Tuesday Tempeh Tacos,
150–151
Weeknight Tempeh &
Vegetable Casserole,
208–209
Thai Curry Noodle Soup, 90–*91*
The Blackout Burger, 185–187
"the Mother" in apple cider
vinegar, 20
The Parmesans, *148*–149
The Physician's Committee
for Responsible Medicine
(PCRM), 248
The Summer Salad, *110*–111
The World Health Organization
(WHO), 4
toasting grains, 27
tofu
All-Day Tofu Scramble,
54–55

Chinese "Fried" Quinoa,
164–165
extra-firm and firm, 17
Greek Salad with Sun-Dried-
Tomato Tofu Feta, *118*–120
New York-Style Baked
Chocolate-Swirl
Cheesecake, 231–233
pressing, 17
silken, 17
Thai Curry Noodle Soup,
90–*91*
Tofu Ricotta, 201
tomato paste tip, 99
tomatoes
Greek Salad with Sun-Dried-
Tomato Tofu Feta, *118*–120
ingredient, 56, 81, 152, 162,
171, 179, 195
Smoky Chickpea Stew with
Cherry Tomatoes & Kale,
97–99
Warming Carrot & Tomato
Soup, *84*–85
tools, 11–12, 60, 75
Toppings
Bacon-ish Bits, 113, 116–*117*
building a bowl, 167
The Parmesans, *148*–149
truffles, 226–*227*
Tuesday Tempeh Tacos, *150*–151
turmeric
Cashew Turmeric Parmesan,
148–149
ingredient, 42, 51, 55, 56, 82,
100, 113, 152, 165, 169, 207
Lemon-Turmeric Bliss Balls,
214–215
nutritional properties, 170
turnips, *88*–89

U
umami flavor, 17
Unforgettable French Onion
Dip, 140–*141*
U.S. Centers for Disease Control
and Prevention (CDC), xiv

V
vegan diet, 8
Vegan Richa's Indian Kitchen,
152
Vegetable Jambalaya, 162–*163*

Vegetable Lasagna & Tofu
Ricotta with House
Marinara, 201–203
vegetables, 4, 167
vinegar, 19–20
vitamin E, 4, 18
Vitamix, 11

W
walnuts
The Blackout Burger, 185–187
Country Date Squares,
219–221
Herbed Cheeze Ball, 144–*145*
ingredient, 63, 171
Mint Chocolate-Caramel
Chews, 222–*223*
Walnut Dressing, 108–*109*
Warm Harvest Salad with
Walnut Dressing, 108–*109*
Weeknight Tempeh & Vegetable
Casserole, *208*–209
Wendel, Brian, 247
white balsamic vinegar, *122*–123
white miso, 93
whole foods
fiber, 3, 4
nutrient density, 3
and oils, 7
phytonutrients, 4
plant-based food groups, 4–6
and sweeteners, 21
and wellness, ix–x, xiv–xv,
xvi, 1, 2
whole grains
Amazing Multigrain Bread,
69–71
brand recommendations, 249
brown rice, 12–13
buckwheat, 13
building a bowl, 167
cooking methods, 26–27
plant-based kitchen, 4–5
quinoa, 13
rolled oats, 13
Wholesome Sweeteners, 249
wine vinegar, red/white, 20, 108,
119, 155, 189, 191, 199

Z
zinc, 18, 190
zucchini, 171